CAMBRIDGE STUDIES
IN ENGLISH LEGAL HISTORY
Edited by
HAROLD DEXTER HAZELTINE, LITT.D., F.B.A.
Of the Inner Temple, Barrister-at-Law;
Downing Professor of the Laws of England in
the University of Cambridge

A MANUAL OF
YEAR BOOK STUDIES

T0370544

[Facsimile of the lower half of p. 5 of the only black-letter edition (1678) of the Year Books of Edward II]

A MANUAL OF
YEAR BOOK STUDIES

BY

WILLIAM CRADDOCK BOLLAND
M.A., LL.D.

OF LINCOLN'S INN, BARRISTER-AT-LAW; LATE SANDARS
READER IN THE UNIVERSITY OF CAMBRIDGE, AND SCHOLAR
OF MAGDALENE COLLEGE, CAMBRIDGE

CAMBRIDGE
AT THE UNIVERSITY PRESS
1925

CAMBRIDGE UNIVERSITY PRESS
Cambridge, New York, Melbourne, Madrid, Cape Town,
Singapore, São Paulo, Delhi, Mexico City

Cambridge University Press
The Edinburgh Building, Cambridge CB2 8RU, UK

Published in the United States of America by Cambridge University Press, New York

www.cambridge.org
Information on this title: www.cambridge.org/9781107635159

First published 1925
First paperback edition 2013

A catalogue record for this publication is available from the British Library

ISBN 978-1-107-63515-9 Paperback

CONTENTS

ILLUSTRATIONS

MEDIEVAL LAW REPORTS

ONE of the principal accomplishments of Western scholarship during the last half-century has been the critical examination of historical materials and their fruitful employment in the reconstruction of the past. In this work English scholars have played a conspicuous rôle. They have devoted their attention to the sources of many branches of history, and have written, on the basis of their studies, works of permanent importance. Prominent among these branches of study is English legal history, the materials of which are remarkably rich and abundant. Deriving its inspiration in large measure from Continental scholarship in the field of law, a new school of English legal historians has come into being whose devotion to historical truth and whose lasting imprint upon historical literature are best typified by the scholarly qualities and literary attainments of Frederic William Maitland. This remarkable lawyer and historian is to be regarded, in fact, as the true founder of the school.

The labours of English legal historians have been chiefly directed to the study of the materials of medieval, as contrasted with modern, English law. Conspicuous among these materials are the medieval law reports—the predecessors of our modern law reports—which are known to-day as the Year Books. Scholars of the last few decades have rescued these old reports from the obscurity into which they had fallen in the course of time; and by their researches they have shown us that as sources of our medieval legal history the Year Books possess an interest and importance unrivalled by any other body of documents.

Among living scholars who have devoted themselves to the editing of Year Books a place of preëminence is held by Dr Bolland: as editor he is, indeed, the legitimate and worthy successor of Horwood, Pike, and Maitland. The stately series of Year Books of the reign of Edward II, published by the Selden Society, bears witness to Dr Bolland's industry and capacity

as an editor and author; and the appearance of a new work by
Dr Bolland is therefore an event of much importance in the
history of Year Book literature. In this book, herewith presented
to the public, there is valuable matter in regard to the bibliography of the Year Books, a subject which has hitherto received
but little consideration. Mr Soule's short article in the *Harvard
Law Review* on "Year Book Bibliography" has been, for a
quarter of a century, almost our only authority. Even the present
volume, as the learned author would be the first to assert, is but
suggestive of the value of such researches: there is still much
work to be done before we shall possess a complete account of
the MSS. and printed editions of the Year Books. Dr Bolland's
book is, however, an illuminating introduction to the subject; and
it ought surely to achieve its main purpose of inspiring younger
legal and historical scholars with a keen interest in the study
of the Year Books and a determination themselves to make
contributions within this realm of investigation. The novel
apparatus provided in Appendix B will now enable beginners
in editorship to resolve the main difficulties incident to the
reading of the MSS. Additional trained editors, and funds for
the publication of their work by the Selden Society, are indeed an urgent necessity of our time. The harm done by the
older printed editions of the Year Books—from Machlinia's
time onwards—is incalculable: historical untruths have been
perpetuated from generation to generation, as the corruption
of the printed text has been carried over into the mass of our
legal and historical writings. What we now need, in fact, is
the re-editing of all the Year Books along the lines laid down
by the Rolls and the Selden Society editions of the Year
Books of the early Edwards; for only after the Year Books
have all been printed in accurate editions will it be possible
to collate them with the older inaccurate editions and hence
to indicate the errors of the past.

Apart from its value as a repository of information and an
inspiration to research, Dr Bolland's book has a further signifi-
cance. Both in England and in America particular attention is
now being paid to English legal history in the education of the
lawyer; in nearly all the leading law schools this subject finds

to-day a place in the curriculum. Evidence of this increasing interest in English legal history is to be found in the fact that the Society of Public Teachers of Law of England and Wales has devised a scheme for instruction in the history of the Year Books and the law embodied in them. When carried into effect this new activity of the Society of Public Teachers of Law will be supplementary to the work of publication long conducted so successfully by the Selden Society. As a basis for instruction, under this new plan, Dr Bolland's present *Manual of Year Book Studies* and his earlier writings will be an invaluable aid to both teacher and student.

It is clear from Dr Bolland's pages not only that the Year Books were originally written for the practical purposes of the legal profession, but that the older printed editions were prepared for the same ends. This is true of Machlinia's editions and also of the editions of some of the later printers. The printed Year Books were those of then recent years: in these the lawyers of the times found the law as then administered by the Courts and which it was essential for them to know. Dr Bolland mentions certain reasons why the Year Books ceased to be read. In addition to these another reason seems to lie in the fact that the law was developing in many directions away from the older common law of the middle age as set forth in the Year Books. Many of the newer rules and principles were embodied in the cases which found their place in the new series of Reports which chronologically followed the Year Books. With this later development the Year Books passed into the category of historical, as contrasted with current and practical, materials. The reasons why students of our day are once more turning their attention to the Year Books are to be sought in that revival of interest in the history of English law to which attention has already been directed. The origins of many of our existing legal rules and institutes are now hidden in the cases reported in the Year Books; and only when these have been brought to light shall we be able to grasp in its entirety the evolution of our law.

Dr Bolland's references to the editions of the Abridgments of the Year Books, as well as recent articles upon this subject by

Dr Holdsworth and Dr Winfield, show us clearly that bibliographical studies by the English legal historian should not be restricted to the Year Books. These studies should embrace, as time goes on, not only the Abridgments, works which fall properly within the scope of Year Book research, but also the other primary and secondary sources of English law. Nor should we neglect the continental development: it would be well for some scholar to turn his thought both to the bibliography of the materials of medieval continental law and to the study of these materials from the point of view of their place in the evolution of continental legal systems. Students of English legal history are too apt to focus their attention upon the insular development, neglecting vaster movements in legal history within Europe as a whole. It is not too much to say that Year Book scholarship would be greatly enriched by a comparison of these early English reports with similar collections of cases which made their appearance in nearly every continental country during the middle ages. We must not lose sight of the fact that decided cases have always played a greater rôle in the evolution of continental law than is sometimes held by students of the Codes. The Reception of Roman and Canon Law, for example, was in large measure the work of the Courts. By an intensive study of the continental collections of medieval cases some scholar would be able to tell us whether these materials are to be treated as reports in the sense in which we regard the Year Books as our early reports, or as books of cases similar to *Bracton's Note Book*, or as accounts of cases like those found in some of our early law books, such as *Brevia Placitata* and *Novae Narrationes*. Such comparative studies would go far to free us from insular habits of mind in dealing with our medieval collections of cases; and they might disclose to us some unexpected relations between the history of the English legal profession and that of the legal profession in continental states. In certain particulars professional modes of thought and processes of work tend to be much the same in all Western countries. It would be surprising indeed if one found that the lawyers of the medieval Continent had not acquired a form of literature very closely allied in essential points to the Year Books of medieval England. The solution of this problem should some day form the subject-matter of an instructive essay by a scholar equally familiar with the history of the law cases of both England and the leading continental countries.

Even if this scholar should study only the English and French cases, he might contribute an illuminating chapter to comparative jurisprudence. He would find that in the thirteenth century —the period in which our own English reporting seems to have its origin—French judges and clerks were making notes of cases that came before the Courts. It would be essential for him to study in detail the pamphlets or *cahiers*, known as the *Olim*, that were made in the thirteenth century by the court clerks John de Montluçon, Nicolas de Chartres, and Peter de Bourges; for the *Olim* embody important decisions of the Parlement of Paris. The *Olim* contain matter copied from the rolls; and yet they are clearly distinguishable from the rolls; they are much more than mere transcripts from the rolls. Even to-day scholars are in dispute—much as English lawyers of our time have debated as to the nature of the early Year Books—upon the question as to whether the *Olim* are to be regarded as official documents or as the private work of the clerks, notes taken down for their own personal use. Extending his researches the investigator would find it instructive to examine the *Anciennes Constitutions du Châtelet* and the *Coutumes Notoires du Châtelet*; for in these early law books—at least the first one of which is the work of a practitioner—he will find accounts of cases decided by the Châtelet, the Court, next in importance to the Parlement of Paris, in which the Provost of Paris administered justice in a little castle—or *châtelet*—upon the right bank of the Seine, at the end of the Pont-au-Change. Nor will the student of early French cases fail to take into account the private work known as the *Assisiae Normanniae*, a collection of the decisions rendered by the King's judges at the assizes held in various towns, such as Caen, Bayeux, and Falaise, between the years 1234 and 1237. In his valuable article on "Early Attempts at Reporting Cases," recently published in the *Law Quarterly Review*, Dr Winfield not only reminds us that the form and purpose of the earlier Year Books differ materially from those of a current law report;

he also suggests that "possibly the embryo of the Year Book lies in some treatise which is not primarily a report at all," and that, inasmuch as our earlier legal literature passed through "tentative stages," the search for the origins of reporting in England should be carried back into the age before the earliest of the Year Books. Early French legal literature also passed through its tentative stages; and the student of its history will find an abundance of materials at his disposal. No doubt many of the earliest collections of French cases bear no real resemblance to the Year Books of Edward I; and yet it may be found that in some instances there is a striking similarity. Clearly there are early law books in France which are much like our own *Brevia Placitata* and *Novae Narrationes*; and in the French works, not less than in the English, there are accounts of judicial decisions. The history of early attempts at reporting law cases in the two countries is not an easy subject of investigation; and the student will be beset at many points with difficulties. One danger he must at all hazards avoid: he must not confuse the official court roll with the unofficial report. It is as necessary to draw this distinction in French legal history as it is in the history of English law. A careful and detailed comparison of French legal literature in the thirteenth and fourteenth centuries with the literature of English law in the same period would at least bring the true facts to light; it would reveal to us the exact nature of the various case-books which played so important a rôle in the medieval legal life of both countries. Investigations in the history of rolls and reports during the thirteenth century should prove to be particularly fruitful in results. In that age, before the legal institutions of France began to differ widely from those of England, one might confidently expect to find, indeed, that the exigencies of legal practice in the two countries led to the production of certain common types of rolls and reports. In our search for the earliest English reports, the predecessors of our Year Books, and in our study of their form and purpose, we may yet discover that our labours can be lightened by a reading of the history of medieval case-books in the regions across the Channel.

H. D. H.

AUTHOR'S PREFACE

THE text of this book reproduces, with some expansions and some compressions, the lectures which I delivered in the University of Cambridge during my tenure of the Sandars Readership in Bibliography[1]. I valued very highly the opportunity which was then given me of speaking at some length of the Year Books in my own University. When Professor Hazeltine suggested that I should edit these lectures, for inclusion in his Series of *Cambridge Studies in English Legal History*, with such additions as I thought might make them more practically useful to students and would-be students of the Year Books, I recognised that an even greater opportunity of doing something which might really advance Year Book Scholarship was being afforded me.

It seemed to me and to others whom I consulted that apart from and in addition to the general story of the Year Books and their origin and descent to us in their present form, as I have tried to tell it in the lectures, some apparatus might be included in this volume which would enable a student to teach himself just so much of the mediaeval scripts in which the Year Books are written and of the contractions which the scribes used as would enable him to make an intelligent beginning of a study of the manuscripts, if he so wished. Nothing of the kind has, so far as I know, been hitherto available, and I have reason to know that the lack of it has been felt and regretted. In furtherance of this purpose I have included in an appendix eleven facsimiles of Year Book manuscripts of various dates, written in various scripts. I have transcribed each of these, expanding in my transcripts everything written *in compendio* in the original, for it would be impossible to reproduce these abbreviated forms

[1] 1922–3.

exactly in ordinary type. If any one, no matter how inexperienced he may be in these studies, will take a little initial trouble in comparing the facsimiles word by word with the transcripts, I do not think that he need be very long before he has gained such a working knowledge of the mediaeval characters and scripts as will grow quickly when he ventures further afield and tries to make his way by his own guidance. Besides these transcripts of the written text I have also given translations of them all; and these translations, I hope, will not be without use to the student. They are not always quite exact or word for word translations, for such, considering the compressed nature of the originals, are often quite impossible, but they are never so free that the text and meaning of the Anglo-Norman original cannot be followed easily in them.

In choosing passages from the original manuscripts for reproduction in facsimile I have not been careful to choose always the most correctly written or the most easily intelligible passages. I have deliberately selected some passages because they show obvious and easily emended mistakes made by the scribes; others because they contain more perplexing errors, errors which could not be at all certainly emended if there were not some other text available for purposes of collation. To show just one instance of this I will refer the student to Plate II. Here we find written what is unmistakably the recognized abbreviation for *non obstante*. *Non obstante* seems to make nonsense of the text. It would have been difficult to say with any confidence what the scribe ought to have written if another text had not given us *neumbre* in the place of *non obstante*. As *neumbre* makes sense, we may be fairly sure that it is the correct reading. Unfortunately we have not always other collatable texts which will help us in like troubles. I have drawn attention in short foot-notes to the transcripts to these textual errors and difficulties. The frontispiece is a facsimile of about half a page of the folio black letter "standard" edition

(1678-1680) of the Year Books, the only edition which contains the Year Books of Edward II. This facsimile reproduces in print the script of Plate IV. Being printed in "record" type, it reproduces more accurately the abbreviated forms of the original manuscript than it is possible to do in ordinary type; and, if for this reason only, will not be without its use to the student.

I will conclude this short Preface with a personal note of thanks, first to the Electors to the Sandars Readership for giving me the opportunity of furthering an interest, to the best of my ability, in the old Year Books in our University, an opportunity of which I was most happy to avail myself for more reasons than one; and, secondly, to Professor Hazeltine and the Syndics of the Cambridge University Press not only for amplifying that opportunity within our own University but for extending its potentialities far further afield.

W.C.B.

1925

I

THE HISTORY AND GENERAL CHARACTERISTICS OF THE YEAR BOOKS

THE Sandars Readership was, according to the terms of the generous founder's gift, created to make provision for the delivery of lectures in Cambridge University on Bibliography, Palaeography, Typography, Book-binding, Book illustration, the Science of Books and Manuscripts and the arts relating thereto. It is obvious that no one lecturer could, during the term of his incumbency, speak adequately on all or on nearly all of these multifarious matters. I shall, I take it, be sufficiently complying with the founder's wishes and intentions if I address myself during these lectures to any of the subjects named within the four corners of the endowment, even though I leave untouched more of those subjects than those with which I actually deal. Still, that leaves your Reader with an embarrassing array of matters from which to make his choice. A truly portentous list of subjects is presented to him. When I showed it to a certain distinguished member of the University, he said to me, with a touch of that caustic wit which he occasionally manifests, "Yes, it looks as though you had to know all about books —except what is inside them." It being taken, then, as a thing of necessity that some limited, and narrowly limited, choice had to be made, what was the choice to be? Through the confusion of the claims or attractions of this and that particular subject, a certain clear call to me, the only clear call, seemed to be sounded in the letter in which the University Librarian[1] informed me of my election to the Readership. "We have," he said, "a fine collection of Year Books in our Library, and I hope that you will have something to tell us about them." There came the call to which I hope to make myself obedient in some useful sort of way. The trouble is that I have already, at one time and another, in one place and another, said and written so much

[1] Francis John Henry Jenkinson, for whose death since these lines were written the whole University grieves: whose friendship was a joy to all those whose happy fortune it was to have it: whose memory is an abiding treasure.

about the Year Books that I stand in much danger of repeating myself. On the other hand, there are certain things which in the present condition of affairs can scarcely be repeated too often or before too many audiences. The claims of the Year Books to be more widely known and studied and to be more, much more, available for the use and study of workers on each and every branch of mediaeval English history, and on other sub-jects, indeed, than history, are amongst these things, for—and this is one of the remarks I am conscious of having made before —there is no other branch of our national literature of which otherwise well-informed people know so little as our old Year Books; though I hope that these books are nowadays getting a little better, a little more widely known, than they have been for some centuries past. If they are not, I am sure that it is not the fault of any undue self-suppression on my own part whenever any opportunity has been granted me of urging their great interest and unique value not only for expert working scholars of almost every kind, but also for that large class of people with literary inclinations who desire to know generally what is to be known of all the many matters touching not only the legal history of their country, but of its social history, of the social conditions of the Middle Age and the relations then existing amongst all the various classes of society; and it is the story of these, with many another one besides, that is hidden away in these old Year Books of which the lettered world of to-day, taken as a whole, knows so little, and by which, because it knows so little, it profits so little. There may be diamonds galore to be had for the gathering a few inches underground close to your own door, but what avails it if you do not know of, if you do not even suspect, their existence? So it is for the most part to-day with our Year Books. Men knew them well once and valued them. Think of the edition after edition of them—of which I shall have something to say at the proper time—which streamed from the press in the sixteenth and seventeenth centuries, and what that continuous stream of editions meant. They would not have been poured out in such numbers unless many people had wanted them, unless those many people who wanted them had also been willing to pay high prices for them and believed that they were getting good value for their money. Why has that once keen interest in the Year Books so woefully withered up and died away in these later centuries, died away so generally that except in some secluded chamber here and there in the Temple of Scholarship practically no memory of them, no recollection of their existence, survives? Why? Men and women still read and love their Chaucer. Gower and Occleve are well enough known by name, at any rate. Historical scholars would deem themselves all insufficiently equipped for their work without a knowledge of the mediaeval chroniclers; but who, outside the scanty band of scholars who have found their way into that inner chamber, knows anything to-day of the Year Books? And the Year Books are in a sense as interesting as Chaucer, and, as I hope to show you, a good deal more trustworthy, a good deal more profitable. It is on record that Serjeant Maynard, who died in 1690, so delighted in the old Year Books that he always carried one with him in his coach to divert himself while he was travelling, and said that he preferred it to any comedy[1]. I suppose that those very printed Year Books themselves were primarily responsible for the oblivion into which they have fallen, or, at any rate, that the people who printed them were. They are a hopeless mass of corruption. These are Maitland's words[2], which I fully adopt and make my own, and vouch my own knowledge of them in warranty of them: "Those who have attempted to read them will know how bad, how incorrigibly bad they are[3]." Though they were read, and read with much profit, by the generations of lawyers and students for whom they were produced, because the men of those generations were steeped to the finger-tips in the lore of the old law and the old procedure, because they knew by intuition, where it is hard for us to guess even after much thought, what the book ought to say, what it meant to say, what it must be taken to say, they could not be read at all by later generations, who, by disuse, had lost the art of reading with any ease the old Gothic character, with its drastic abbreviations, in which these books were printed, and, except in the case of a few experts, had never acquired that intimate knowledge of the old law and the old procedure, the

---

[1] Roger North's *Lives of the Norths* (1826), I, p. 27.
[2] *Collected Papers*, I, p. 484.
[3] Selden Society's *Year Book Series*, I, p. xxi.

trained instinct to read in what was there that which was not there, what was, perhaps, the very opposite of what was there. No ordinary man of letters, no ordinary lawyer or law student could reasonably be expected to read through the Year Books in that ragged Gothic dress, marred and disfigured by every kind of corruption of which the mediaeval printer was capable, in which alone they were to be found. And so men ceased to read them, and soon forgot all about them, even their very existence. Primarily, I said, the Year Books themselves were perhaps responsible for the oblivion into which they have fallen. The word "primarily" necessarily infers some second or auxiliary reason. And the second operative cause, I think, through which the Year Books fell into disuse and oblivion was this. At the time when the old printed texts were becoming unintelligible one thinks that it ought to have been the duty of some one, of the Government, of the Universities—there were only two in those days—of the Inns of Court, to make provision for a new edition of them which could be read with ease by the man who was repelled by the mere sight of the Gothic character, an edition which should at least have corrected the more glaring of the manifold corruptions of the earlier text, an edition which should not have made virtually impossible demands upon a reader who tried to understand it. And so, for one reason and another, anything like serious study of the Year Books died out, and only some legal bookworm here and there found his occasional way into that array of tall folios and large quartos which would hardly have been missed from our libraries if their places had been filled with dummy volumes. And after this fashion the Year Books passed out of generally known literature. But the resurrection was to come, though it was to be a tardy one and sluggish, and even now is scarcely more than in its first painful throes to get itself accomplished. And this is the story of its beginning. I am afraid that the man who shall be privileged to tell the story of its full completion is not yet out of the nursery, even if he be already within it. So long ago as 1614 Lord Bacon had written of the Year Books:

As these Reports are more or less perfect, so the Law itself is more or less certain, and indeed better or worse. Whereupon a conclusion may be made, that it is hardly possible to confer upon this Kingdom a greater benefit than if his Majesty should be pleased that these books also may be purged and reviewed[1].

But nothing came of that appeal. In the early part of the year 1800 the state of the Public Records was brought under the consideration of the House of Commons, and thereupon a Select Committee was appointed "to enquire into the state of the Public Records of Great Britain, and of such other Public Instruments, Rolls, Books and Papers as they should think proper; and to report to the House the nature and condition thereof; together with what they should judge fit to be done for the better arrangement, preservation and more convenient use of the same." This Committee sought information and advice from the custodians throughout the country of documents coming under the above-named heads. Besides the Public Offices, the Universities, the Colleges thereof, the Inns of Court, and all the great Libraries of the realm were asked to make reports and offer suggestions. In June, 1800, the Committee produced a first report. As, in making its recommendations, it appears to have attached much weight to the return made by the Society of Lincoln's Inn, on the great erudition and ability of which it lays emphasis, it will not be out of place to give some extracts from that return here. It is dated 26th May, 1800, and is signed on behalf of the Benchers by Mr Sylvester Douglas, then Master of the Library. Speaking of the Year Books, this return from Lincoln's Inn says:

Whatever may have been the nature of the Authority under which those Books were compiled, and whatever the particular Description of the Compilers (concerning which there seems to be a considerable Diversity of Opinion), they are universally considered as containing Official and Authentic Accounts of the Arguments and Decisions in the most important Causes which came before the Chief Tribunals of this Country, from a very early Period down to the general Introduction of Printing; about which Time certain eminent Judges and Lawyers, as Keilway, Moore, Benloe, Dyer, Plowden, &c. began, without any Special Appointment or Duty, to make similar Compilations, with a view of committing them to the Press. Such a valuable

---

[1] "A Memorial touching the Review of Penal Laws and the Amendment of the Common Law" (*The Letters and the Life of Francis Bacon*, edited by James Spedding, 1869, v, p. 85).

monument of practical Law and Jurisprudence as the Year Books, probably, does not exist in any other Country. But,

1. In the printed Editions of these important Annals, there are many Chasms and Interruptions in the Series of the Years.

2. The printed Copies abound with many Imperfections of other Sorts. The Cases, Arguments and Judgments are not so fully stated in them as they are to be met with in some of the Manuscripts, because those Editions were (as it should seem) made from other Manuscripts less complete; the Editors not having had the Means or Industry, at least, of resorting to those which were more full and accurate.

3. They are printed so close, so many of the Manuscript Abbreviations are retained, and there is so little Separation into Paragraphs, or Distinction between what is said by the Counsel, and what by the Judges, that it often requires the Experience and Sagacity of a legal Antiquary, and generally much more Time than the practising Lawyer can bestow, to read, or rather to decypher, the Passages to which there is Occasion to refer.

4. There is no General well-digested Index to them[1].

Touching the Year Books the Select Committee made the following recommendations:

Your Committee strongly recommend that the series of those Books from Edward the First to Henry the Eighth should be completed by printing those hitherto unpublished; of which there are several extant in the Libraries of Lincoln's Inn, the Inner Temple and the British Museum; and also by reprinting the rest from more correct copies, as those which are already in print are known to be in many instances incorrect and erroneous. A General Index to the whole would be a very necessary addition to such a work, which forms so valuable a monument of our practical Jurisprudence in its earliest ages [2].

The old black-letter editions included no reports at all of either Edward I's reign or of Richard II's. Many of the years of Edward III had been omitted, and at least one term of Henry VI for which there is manuscript authority. The effect of the Committee's representation was, therefore, that reports of all those unprinted years and terms which I have just named should be printed for the first time, and that a revised and corrected edition of all the others should be prepared and published. Nothing at

---

[1] *First Report on Public Records* (1800), p. 381. For further instructive extracts from this return see Appendix A, p. 109 below.

[2] *Op. cit.* p. 16.

all was done for some sixty or seventy years. After the lapse of that time the then Master of the Rolls found himself able to take steps for doing something, but only for doing very much less than the Committee had said ought to be done. Mr A. J. Horwood, a barrister of the Inner Temple, was commissioned to edit the hitherto unpublished Year Books of Edward I—no Year Book at all of this reign, you will remember, had as yet been printed—and afterwards to fill up the gap existing in the black-letter editions between the tenth and seventeenth years of Edward III. Nothing at all was said about the missing books of Richard II's reign. Mr Horwood died before his task was completed, having issued only five volumes, which included reports of the twentieth, twenty-first and twenty-second years of Edward I and of the years 30–35, inclusive, of the same reign. He left unfinished at the time of his death a volume which included the reports of the whole of the eleventh year and of the first three terms of the twelfth year of Edward III. His unfinished work was then taken up by Mr L. O. Pike, a barrister of Lincoln's Inn, who completed, in successive volumes, the assigned task of filling up the gaps existing between the tenth and seventeenth years and between the eighteenth and twenty-first years of Edward III. Mr Pike also re-edited and published the reports of the seventeenth and eighteenth years of the same reign. His last volume, containing reports of 20 Edward I, was not published until 1911, though the text and translation was out of his hands in May, 1908. The reason of this delay was that new printers had at that time been selected by the Government to do the work, and they were necessarily unfamiliar with its nature. Soon after the preliminary difficulties arising from this reason had been surmounted, the Company went into liquidation and all progress ceased for some three years. And this was the end of the Government's encouragement of Year Book study and scholarship. Nothing had been done, nothing had been even said, about the Richard II books, though the necessary manuscripts were then awaiting, as they are still awaiting, an editor, and, except for the re-editing by Mr Pike of two years of Edward III, a deaf ear was turned to the Committee's recommendation that the whole series of the "incorrect and erroneous" black-letter editions should be re-edited. This all too short series of Year Books edited by Mr Horwood and Mr Pike is part of the official publications generally known as the Rolls Series. Their full title is *Chronicles and Memorials of Great Britain and Ireland during the Middle Ages*. While Mr Pike was still continuing his work the Selden Society had been founded, largely by the efforts of Maitland. Its professed purpose was to advance the knowledge and to encourage the study of the History of English Law. It was through this Society that Maitland hoped to carry out "one of the great undertakings of his life[1]," a new edition of some part of the Year Books. As the surviving Year Books of Edward I's reign, of which there are not very many, and the hitherto un-edited years of Edward III had been put by the Master of the Rolls into the competent hands of Mr Horwood and Mr Pike, the Selden Society determined to commence its work on the Year Books with a new and fair edition of those of the reign of Edward II. The text of the old black-letter edition is exceedingly corrupt. It is made from a single manuscript only; and there were several others, the existence of which was known to the Selden Society, which supplied many additional cases, besides enabling an editor to correct many of the errors and corruptions in the one text which the old edition followed, or was supposed to follow, though it did not, but added generously to the already sufficiently abundant lapses of the original. Maitland was him-self the first editor, using and collating nine different manuscripts. Four volumes in all he was able to publish before his sadly premature death in 1906. Since then the Society, with the assistance of various editors, has published fifteen more volumes in its Year Book Series. These, however, are not all consecutive volumes, the editions and publication of certain volumes in their due order having been hindered by one cause and another. One of these causes, it may be interesting to note, being the German air-raids which necessitated, for safety's sake, the temporary removal from London of various essential records and their inaccessible immurement within Bodmin Gaol. The Selden Society now remains the only body which is doing any-

[1] *Frederic William Maitland*, by H. A. L. Fisher, p. 163.

thing towards giving the world a tolerable edition of the Year Books, and it is a purely private society of scholars receiving neither financial assistance nor encouragement of any sort from the Government, and its own means are narrowly limited. These things being so, the probability of scholars of either this generation or the next having what Maitland declared was "the first and indispensable preliminary" to a sufficient history of our law, "a new, a complete, a tolerable edition of the Year Books[1]," seems lamentably small. What I have said will suffice for the moment as a mere outline sketch of the bibliography of the Year Books, which I will amplify later at the proper time.

It will be expedient now to say something of the nature and of the contents of the Year Books, for, as I have already remarked, there is no other branch of our national literature of which the great majority of people who do know much about our literature know so little as they know of the Year Books; and I hope that if there be any who are conscious that they could not here and now give anything like a lucid account of them they will not feel over-abashed, seeing that I have given them such excellent reasons why they cannot fairly be expected to know much about them. On the other hand, there are those who do know a great deal about the Year Books, who have used them, so far as they are available, in their studies and know as well as I do what they are and what they are worth. These will forgive me for repeating here what they have learned for themselves. I will be as brief as I can be consistently with my purpose, which is that when I come to speak in detail of the bibliography of the Year Books I may not find myself speaking of a class of books of the nature and contents of which anyone who listens to me shall be without that amount of knowledge which is necessary if I am to hope to succeed in awakening and maintaining in them some real interest in my subject. Besides Bibliography, Palaeography is another matter of which, while strictly confining myself within the scheme of this Readership, I may speak. Bibliography, in the modern acceptation of the word, deals with printed books, Palaeography concerns itself with manuscripts; and the Year

---

[1] Pollock and Maitland, *History of English Law* (2nd ed.), I, p. xxxv.

Books are both, and any dissertation upon them must fall under both these heads. I will not attempt any formal definition of the Year Books. They lend themselves no better to formal definition than Cleopatra did to description. Like her, too, they are of infinite variety. And, indeed, I am less anxious to give you, even if I could, a completely satisfying definition or description of them than to tell you enough about them to sharpen your curiosity to know more; to induce you to go to them yourselves so far as they are yet available for general study. What, then, are these old Year Books of ours; who wrote them and when and why? For the beginning of them, for the first beginning, at any rate, that is now known to us, you must go back to the earlier years of Edward I; perhaps even still further back. You must go inside William Rufus's great hall at Westminster, to that corner of it where the Court of Common Bench is sitting. You will see the Justices of the Bench, in varying number, vested in scarlet robes and wearing the coif on their heads, the coif which marked them as being of the Serjeant's degree, sitting on a raised dais. If the Chief Justice be present he will sit in the centre of the group. On the wall, over their heads, are three shields in their proper heraldic colours. That on the dexter side bears the arms of Edward the Confessor; the centre shield those of England and France quarterly; the sinister one those of England alone. The clerks of the Court are seated at a table, covered with a green cloth, which stands immediately below the Justices' dais. A couple of ushers, carrying staves, are ready for whatever duties may be laid upon them. Serjeants are standing round the table. There do not seem to have been seats provided for any but the Judges and the clerks. Clerks, Serjeants and ushers are all wearing parti-coloured robes. There was a sort of box or stand, known as the Crib, on one side of the Court, provided for the use of the apprentices and students, where they might follow the proceedings in Court and learn their business by the time they should receive the Serjeant's coif and gain the right of audience, which in the Court of Common Bench was exclusively the Serjeants' privilege. The apprentices were those whom to-day we should call barristers. They had the right of audience in the Court of King's Bench, but they were present in the Court of Common Bench as learners rather than as practitioners. In this connexion I may mention that an ancient petition[1] to Edward II has survived in which the King is asked to order his Treasurer and the Chief Justice of the Common Bench to allow his apprentices of the common law to make a second crib on the other side of the Court where they might stand for their instruction as in the Crib already existing. Such is something like what you would have seen if you had gone into Westminster Hall in the time of Edward I or Edward II when the Court of Common Bench was sitting. The ancient illumination[2] on which I have relied for my description is of a somewhat later date, but I daresay that it gives us with fair accuracy the scene of earlier years.

I said just now that you would see the Justices sitting on the Bench in varying number. I ought now to say something a little more definite on that point. The number of the Justices of the Common Bench varied greatly at different times. Before Edward II's time there were, so far as I can discover, usually three. Edward II gradually appointed additional Justices. In the third year of his reign he issued, jointly with his Council, an ordinance[3] decreeing that in future there should be six Justices for the Common Bench; and the reason given for this increase of the number of the Justices was that "it is necessary to have two places owing to the number of pleas, now greater than ever." The Justices appointed by this ordinance were Master William of Bereford, "who is Chief by the King's command," Sir Lambert of Trikingham, Sir Hervey of Stanton, Master Harry Scrope, Sir John of Benstede and Sir William of Bourn. There are some points in this ordinance on which I will say a word or two. In the first place I may say that I do not know why the Chief Justice is designated in this ordinance of 1310 Master William of Bereford, seeing that in a Parliamentary writ of 1302[4] he is already styled Sir William of Bereford. Sir William of Bourn does not appear ever actually to have sat

---

[1] Happily discovered by Mr G. J. Turner. See Selden Society's *Year Book Series*, IV, p. xli.   [2] See *Archaeologia*, XXXIX.
[3] *Calendar of Close Rolls* (1307–1313), p. 231.
[4] *Parliamentary Writs*, I, p. 131 (No. 63).

on the Bench. Fines were always levied before the full Court, and there is no record of Sir William of Bourn ever having been present at the levying of a fine. We must suppose, therefore, that for some reason or another his appointment never took effect, or that it was immediately revoked by the King. Neither is there any record as to this "second place," which was, I suppose, what we should call to-day a second division or Court of the Common Bench. Benstede does not appear at all in the Year Book reports of the time, and Trikingham, at first, only very casually. Probably these two sat as a separate Court at Westminster merely to try issues which had been formally laid before the Justices of the first division; and this work would be entirely without interest to the reporters. It seems fairly certain, then, that there were only six Justices of the Common Bench effectively appointed under this ordinance, and there do not appear to have been more than six during the rest of Edward II's reign. In 7 Edward III there were seven, in 11 and 12 Edward III there were eight, and in the Trinity term of 14 Edward III there were nine. After that date there were usually only five. For a time, at the beginning of Henry VI's reign, there were again seven. Afterwards there were seldom more than five until the years subsequent to 27 Henry VI, when the number of the Justices varied from time to time, but never exceeded eight. At the end of Edward IV's reign there were only four, and I think that there were never more than four all through the reign of Henry VII.

When we have looked round and seen what is to be seen, let us listen to what is to be heard. An action is being tried. Half a dozen Serjeants, even more, may be engaged in it on one side and the other. They are talking one against another. They do not seem always to have been over-courteous to each other, nor always over-respectful to the Justices[1]. Even if a Justice disagreed with a brother-Justice sitting on the Bench with him, he did not hesitate to tell him that such and such an interpretation of the law had been judicially laid down by one who was wiser than he. Into the heated debate of the Serjeants the Justices

[1] Serjeant Grene, *e.g.*, told Kelleshull J. that what he said was not law. *Year Books* (Rolls Series), 19 Edward III, p. 137.

intervene occasionally, to give a ruling on the admissibility of a plea, to give their recollections of something that had happened within their own experience that seemed to have a bearing on the actual case before them, to tell a story after the nature of a parable, to quote the bible, the classics or a continental *brocard*. And the Serjeants are quite as ready-tongued. They all have the resources of the highest culture of the Middle Age to draw upon; and in that hall to which I have taken you the most highly cultured life of the Middle Age is finding its fullest expression in argument and repartee, in illustration and criticism, in apt quotation, in jibe and sarcasm. And as the Serjeants state their different cases you will hear stories of all sorts of people, told in explaining why this action or the other has been brought; told in explaining, on the other hand, why it ought never to have been brought and how entirely without justification it is; stories of all manner and degrees of people from Kings and Archbishops and Earls to farm labourers and villeins; stories of the relations and dealings of these people with each other, illustrating the social conditions of the time; stories of what people ate and drank and how much, and what were the current prices of all sorts of things, from cattle-sheds to apple-trees, from wine to herrings and eggs. You will hear much of ecclesiastics—you will remember that at this time England was sown thick throughout its length and breadth with Abbeys and Priories and religious houses of all kinds—of their quarrels amongst themselves and with their neighbours, of their disputes about patronage and tithes and debts and the like, and, sometimes, of their extremely overbearing treatment of their lowly dependents. Something you will hear of the surgical methods of the time and of the contemporary doctrine of professional negligence in cases where, instead of the hoped-for cure being effected, the patient's condition grew worse[1]. Something, may be, you will hear of the peculiar curative system which appears to have been in vogue for the treatment of madmen; will perhaps hear a witness say, as though he were relating a quite ordinary incident: "he went mad and was doing a great deal of harm. So I and his

---

[1] See *e.g.* Year Books, 41 Edward III, p. 19, case 13; and the report of a surgeon's action to recover his fees in Hil. 48 Edward III, p. 6, case 11.

other relations seized him and bound him and took him into a house and thrashed him with a stick[1]." Remembering the present immunity of counsel from all liability for negligence, you may be surprised to hear one of the Justices saying that if a Serjeant undertakes to plead a cause and does not or, in pleading it, departs from his instructions, he is liable in an action for damages[2]. Nor does it sound less strange to the modern barrister to hear that his mediaeval predecessors were entitled to sue for their fees. If a litigant retained the services of counsel he must pay him whatever fee he had agreed to pay him, and if he did not his counsel had a right of action against him for the recovery of it. Now, as everyone knows, counsel cannot be sued for negligence nor can he sue for unpaid fees. I am afraid I cannot say when the present law on these matters first became established or how; but when Sir John Davys first printed his Reports in 1615 he sets out plainly in his Introduction that the law as to counsels' fees was the same in his time as it is to-day, and he says nothing to lead his readers to suppose that he knew it had ever been otherwise. And therein he was more cautious than Mr Forsyth, the author of the classic *Hortensius*, who declares that "In England the rule has always been that which is here laid down by Sir John Davys. A barrister has no legal right to a fee[3]." But the case in 30 Henry VI[4] to which I have referred seems to show that this statement is incorrect. The liability for negligence and the right to recover fees probably became extinguished at the same time, sometime between 1451 and a date long before 1615, the one cancelling the other. From the report of the case cited we gather that the ordinary fee of

[1] *Liber Assisarum*, 22 Edward III, p. 98, case 65.
[2] Year Books, 14 Henry VI, p. 18.   [3] *Op. cit.* (ed. 1849), p. 422.
[4] "Il ad dit en son ple qe il retenut un W. Moile apprentis estre a counsel …cest parole *retenuit* enclude en soy mesme une cause daction envers cesty qe fist le reteiner pur les deniers a luy promis sur le reteiner. Et si nul denier en certein soit a luy promis donqes il aura tant en comon droit luy done come a Serjeant xl *d.* et al attorney xx *d.* decesty qe luy retenut." Year Books, Mich. 30 Henry VI, p. 9 [B], case 1.
    In the Plea Roll of the Common Bench for Mich. 8 Edward II (No. 207), r. 170 *d*, it is stated that nine shillings and twenty pence are to be paid for the *feodum* of the King's Clerk, the *feodum* of the Cyrographer and the *stipendium* of the Serjeant (*narrator*) upon the making of a cyrograph of the note of a fine.

a Serjeant in the reign of Henry VI was forty pence. Later on it seems to have been an angel, a gold coin which varied in value from six shillings and eight pence to ten shillings; and there was an old riddle which asked "Why is a Serjeant like Balaam's ass? Because he won't speak until he has seen an angel." From which we may perhaps gather that in those days counsels' fees were usually paid in advance. Although the Serjeants alone had the right of audience in the Common Bench, the Justices of that Bench could grant that right to the Apprentices of the Law in the absence of Serjeants; and the report which tells us this gives us also some interesting and authoritative information as to the power of the Justices to deprive counsel of his right of audience[1].

You will hear how sometimes in those robust days even the officers of the Court took to open brawling in Court, and sometimes with fatal consequences. In 1322 two of the clerks of the King's Chancery quarrelled and fought in Westminster Hall, while the King himself was present in some room close at hand. One of these clerks killed the other, and short shrift was given him. He was immediately taken away and hanged: *statim suspensus est*. Even in Parliament itself, in that same year, William de la Souche and the Lord J. de Grey drew swords on each other in the King's presence; but before any harm appears to have been done the King ordered them both to be arrested and imprisoned. You will hear, too, as you listen to certain cases to which an Abbot or Prior is a party, a phrase that sounds rather oddly in modern ears. A man of religion, that is a professed religious, cannot change his mind. I do not know when this principle of mediaeval law was first established or how it became established, but as it worked out in, so far as I know, its only practical application, for the benefit and advantage of the diocesan bishops, it is not unlikely that the bishops had something to do with it. This is how the principle, which was completely allowed by the Courts, worked in practice. Abbots and Priors were patrons of many ecclesiastical benefices. An Abbot presents his nominee to the Bishop for admission and institution to a vacant living. Upon inquiry the nominee is found to be not

[1] Year Books, 11 Edward IV, p. 3 [B], case 4.

qualified to hold the benefice; he is, perhaps, under the canonical age, or he is not of sufficient learning, or, may be, he is married. As the patron, being a man of religion, cannot change his mind, he cannot depart from his first unfortunate choice and present another nominee to the Bishop. The Bishop waits for six months, and then himself presents to the living by lapse of time. As you know, the religious and secular clergy of the Middle Age did not love each other over-enthusiastically. You will hear now and again of many peculiar and interesting local customs which are not to be found recorded in any existing costumals, such as the custom of Lincoln by which when a man had had two wives the issue of the first wife took three-quarters of his estate of inheritance, and the issue of the second took the other quarter. One of the manuscript Year Books, by the way, speaks of the case where the man had three wives, but makes the same division of the estate between the issue of the first and second wives, and leaves nothing over for the issue of the third wife. I suppose that it mentions the third wife for the purpose of showing that her issue took nothing. Then you will hear of those local customs by which children attained full age much sooner than they did under the general common law of the land. At Scarborough, for example, fifteen years constituted full age[1]. The custom of Ipswich was that a person was of full age when he could count and weigh and measure cloth, and when that custom was pleaded at Westminster in 1304 the Court allowed it; but when, some thirty-five years later a similar custom said to be observed at Hereford, that a man could sell his land when he could measure an ell and count up to twelve pence, was pleaded, the Court ruled it a bad custom and contrary to law, on the ground that one man may be twenty years' old before he knows how to measure an ell, while another knows when he is seven. But Bridport gives us the strangest example of premature attainment of full age. By the custom of Bridport, we are told, an heir was of full age on the day he was born. And that was a fact officially found and recorded by the King's Escheator[2]. In the manor of Abingdon

---

[1] Year Books, 16 Edward II, p. 478.
[2] I do not get this from the Year Books, but from the *Inquisitions*, 53 Henry III, No. 10.

land was held by one or other of two different systems of tenure. I hesitate about giving you the names of these tenures, for our manuscripts do not agree upon them, and it is obvious that the scribes were trying to write different and, to them, unintelligible words of which they had never before heard. Tenants of land under one of these tenures had to pay a penny to the Abbot of Abingdon, who was lord of the manor, every time they brewed beer—and this penny, the Year Books tell us, was called the Colchester penny[1]. The manuscripts which I have seen agree in saying that it was so called, but as the connexion between Colchester in Essex and the Abbot of Abingdon in Berkshire is not apparent, one suspects some corruption in our texts. The actual words are "pur chescum bracyne il durra Labbe un dener qest appelle Colcestre penny." A "cester" (*sextarius*) was a liquid measure, and a "cester" of beer was not an uncommon toll payable by private brewers to their lord[2]. Probably an early transcriber carelessly wrote "Colcestre" for "cestre," and his mistake was perpetuated by subsequent copyists. Another explanation is quite plausible. The letters "c" and "t" were often confused through their great similarity in mediaeval writing. What was originally written "tol cestre," *i.e.* the toll of a cester, might easily get itself copied as "colcestre," and so we might get "un dener qest appelle Colcestre penny." Beer was continually coming to the front in those mediaeval days, though, indeed, it is fairly in evidence in these present ones[3]. But it does not get itself into chronicles and records to-day in quite the same persistent way as it did in the Middle Age. When Judges go on circuit they do not now straightway send a commission of four knights to all the taverns in each town they visit to test by personal

---

[1] See Year Books, Hil. 12 Edward II, p. 368 and Hale MS. 139, fo. 172 (Lincoln's Inn).

[2] Amongst the customs of an Essex Manor in 1328 was the following: "Every copieholder that doeth brewe bere or ale to sell shall paye yerely in the moneth of harvest one penye called Cestre penye." *Essex Review*, XIII, p. 203.

[3] As far back as the earlier half of the thirteenth century the fame of English beer had reached the Court of Rome. "Et adversarius [*sc.* Robertus Clipstone]: Pater sancte [*sc.* Innocent IV] nos didicimus in scholis et haec est opinio magistrorum nostrorum quod non currit praescriptio contra iura episcopalia. Et dominus papa: Certe et tu et magistri tui multum bibistis de cerevisia Anglicana quando haec didicistis." *Chronicles of Evesham* (Rolls Series), p. 189.

trial the drink sold at each and every one of them, which the Year Books make plain was the invariable custom whenever the mediaeval Justices went into the country to hold an Eyre. "Scotales" and "festales" and "church ales" and other "ales" were the common custom of the land. The custom of "scotales" was so much abused that one of the articles of the Eyre was directed against those who so abused them[1]. There is no doubt that our ancestors drank more than generously according to all modern standards. The actions about corrodies give us plentiful evidence of this. A corrody I may just say, as it is not a term in common use to-day, was a grant of board, lodging, clothing and all necessaries in a religious house. The King was entitled to nominate to a corrody in every religious house of royal foundation; but other people had also a right to nominate. These grants were made in specific terms. They did not leave it to the monastery to give to the beneficiary just what it chose. Disputes as to these corrodies not infrequently gave rise to actions in the Courts, where the terms of the corrody were stated, and from them we gather much interesting information as to what was considered in mediaeval times a reasonable provision of board and lodging for different classes of people. Edward III granted a corrody to an officer of the Royal Wardrobe. The beneficiary was to have a daily allowance of six gallons of ale. There has been preserved an account of "the goodly provision" made for "the great feast at the inthronization of the reverend Father in God George Neville, Archbishop of York and Chancellor of England in the sixth year of the reign of King Edward the Fourth[2]." Three hundred tuns of ale were provided, a hundred tuns of wine, and a pipe of hippocras, which was merely wine spiced. The old glossaries tell us that a tun contained 252 gallons and that a pipe was half a tun. The Archbishop's "goodly provision," therefore, works out at 75,600 gallons of ale and 25,376 gallons of wine. Even Queen Elizabeth considered two gallons of ale only a proper daily allowance for the eight children who sang in the Chapel Royal in St James's Palace. I do not think I need

[1] "De parvis balliuis et quibuscunque facientibus cereuisium quod vocatur scotale quandoque festale ut extorqueant pecuniam a sequentibus hundredum et eorum subditis." See *Year Book Series* (Selden Society), v, p. 32.

[2] Warner's *Antiquitates Culinariae* (1791), pp. 93–106.

add any more to establish my point that our mediaeval ancestors drank generously. Prohibition was only known to them as the name of a certain writ which had nothing to do with either wine or beer. That they were prepared to take pretty strong measures to get these when they wanted them would have been made plain to you if you had been in Court when a certain action for trespass was being tried in Edward III's time[1]. A man wanted a drink late at night, and he went to a tavern to get it. It was so late that when he arrived he found the tavern closed. Possibly he had anticipated this, and so he had thoughtfully provided himself with an axe in case it might be useful in clearing away difficulties. He proceeded to batter the closed door with it. The noise awoke the landlady. She put her head out of a window and told the roysterer to be off about his business. The man then struck at the landlady's head with his axe, but she avoided the blow. How in the end she got rid of the man, whether she gave him what he wanted or did not, I cannot tell you; but she did bring an action of trespass against him. The jury very oddly found that, as the woman had sustained no hurt, no harm had been done and that there was, consequently, no trespass. But the Court refused to accept the jury's conclusions. They said that a great deal of harm had been done, and they bade the jury at once to assess the landlady's damages; and the jury promptly said that they were ten marks.

Nowadays you do not hear published the banns of marriage of a bride of three years old and a bridegroom of seven, but in mediaeval times you might have done, and would not, I suppose, have expressed any surprise if you had. As you listen to the cases being tried in the Court of Common Bench in those far-off years you will see of what trouble and doubt, if of nothing else, these premature marriages were to the parents. Then, as now, twelve and fourteen were respectively the common law ages of consent to marriage for wife and husband; and until they had attained those respective ages no one could say whether they were effectively and permanently married or not. As each came to the age of consent he or she might void the marriage. The real difficulty as we hear it raised in the Court was this.

[1] *Liber Assisarum*, 22 Edward III, p. 99, case 60.

If the husband die before the wife reach consenting age, were they ever so effectively married that the widow was entitled to dower?—you will hear this question raised not infrequently as you sit in the mediaeval courts and listen to what is going on. In process of time the Court made some rough sort of rule that a wife who was nine years old when her husband died was entitled to dower. But here fresh difficulties arose. How was it to be proved, in the case of a very young widow, that she had reached that age? There was no registration of births, and in ordinary life no one seems to have thought of making a memorandum in writing of the birth of a new member of his family. Sometimes the Court was asked to settle the question of a person's age by actual inspection; but that was a responsibility which not all Justices were willing to accept; and Chief Justice Cavendish, when asked in 1373 to determine whether a woman was of full age or under age, declared that there was no man in England who could surely say whether a woman is of full age or not, "for," said he, "there are women of thirty who try to make themselves look as though they were only eighteen[1]." Witnesses were sometimes brought up to Westminster to testify of their own knowledge as to the age of a person born in the neighbourhood where they lived. They were always cross-examined as to how they came to remember the date of the birth, and they usually said that it happened about the same time as something else of which the date was fairly identifiable. I remember an interesting and rather odd reason which a certain witness gave in support of his statement that an heir to land was of the full age of twenty-one years. This heir, he said, had a sister whom he, the witness, was on the point of marrying twenty-one years previously, but, because the parties could not at the last moment agree, he married someone else "at the Feast of the Purification twenty-one years ago." But he does not seem, from so much of his testimony as has survived, to have connected the heir's birth either with his own broken engagement or his apparently hasty marriage with someone else, but I suppose that we must infer that the heir was in existence at the time of the witness's engagement to his sister.

You will be reminded, as you linger in these old Courts, that

[1] Year Books, Hil. 50 Edward III, p. 6, case 12.

leprosy was once a common thing in England, a thing of terror; that a leper could not be allowed to mix with other men; that if dealings must be had with one they must be had in the open air with plenty of room between the leper and the sound man. A leper, may be, was a party to an action. He, above all men, must appoint an attorney to represent him in Court. The ordinary man appointed his attorney inside the Court, but no leper could be allowed to do that. When it was intimated to the Justices that some leper was a litigant, they directed a clerk of the Court to go outside and receive the leper's nomination of an attorney and bring it to them[1]. But though a leper was not only allowed but forced to appoint an attorney to represent him in Court, a deaf and dumb litigant was apparently not allowed to appoint an attorney. He or she must appear *in propria persona*; and it is as difficult to understand how one so afflicted could do justice to his case as it is to understand why he should have been denied the assistance of an attorney. I have come across no report of an actual case in which either of the parties was deaf and dumb, but there is a short report in a Lincoln's Inn manuscript Year Book[2] to the effect that in the Easter term of 8 Edward III a Serjeant came to the bar of the Court and asked

[1] 30 Edward I, p. 115 (Rolls Series). According to Bracton (fo. 421 *a*) leprosy in a plaintiff was a ground for a peremptory exception to his action, but we gather from the case mentioned in the text that, unless formal exception were actually taken, a leper was a competent plaintiff. The following writ *de leproso amovendo* may not be out of place here: "Rex maiori et vicecomitibus Londonie salutem. Quia accepimus quod I. de H. leprosus existit et inter homines civitatis predicte communiter conversatur et cum eis tam in locis publicis quam privatis communicat et se ad locum solitarium prout moris est ad ipsum pertinet transferre recusat ad grave damnum hominum predictorum et propter contagionem morbi predicti periculum manifestum: nos huiusmodi periculo prout ad nos pertinet precavere et super premissis quod iustum est et usitatum fieri volentes vobis precepimus quod assumptis vobiscum aliquibus discretis et legalibus hominibus de civitate predicta non suspectis, qui de persona prefati I. et huiusmodi morbo notitiam habent meliorem, ad ipsum I. accedatis et ipsum in presentia predictorum hominum faciatis diligenter videri et examinari. Et si ipsum leprosum esse inveneritis ut predictum est tunc ipsum honestiori modo quo poteritis a communione hominum predictorum amoveri et se ad locum solitarium ad habitandum ibidem prout moris est transferre faciatis indilate ne per huiusmodi communem conversationem suam hominibus predictis damnum vel periculum eveniat quovis modo." *Register of Writs* (1687), fo. 267.

[2] "*Trewithe* vint a la barre et pria pur vne femme surde et muette qe el purra faire attourne ou gardien a suyre pur li en ple de terre leqel qe la court verra qe soit affaire et la curt nel voleit pas graunter mes suy en propre persone si el voudre." Hale MS. 137 (2), fo. 5.

that a deaf and dumb woman might appoint an attorney or a guardian to sue for her in a plea of land. The Court refused permission, and said curtly that she might sue *in propria persona* if she liked[1]. But I take it that even a deaf and dumb plaintiff might do that without any permission from anyone. This ruling must have made it impossible for this woman to prosecute her action; and it is easy to understand why we do not seem to have any reports of actions by or against deaf and dumb parties. But a litigant who was dumb only, and could hear what was said and give an intelligent assent to it, was allowed to appoint an attorney and even to wage his law in person[2].

We may hap upon some interesting little incidents when a criminal is hoping to save his neck by claiming benefit of clergy without sufficient justification. In days not very long before the date of our earliest surviving Year Books the King's Courts had no jurisdiction to entertain a criminal charge against anyone who had been admitted into any of the orders of the Church, even into the lowest of the minor orders. It was sufficient for such an one to say that he was a clerk and that he could not or would not make any answer in a lay court; and some official of the Bishop would come forward and claim the right of the Bishop's Court to try him; that is, of course, where the Bishop was satisfied or affected to be with the man's claim to clergy. In those earlier days the Court would straightway deliver the prisoner to the Bishop's official, and would themselves make no inquest touching his guilt or innocence. But before the date of our earliest Year Books this simple procedure had become more complicated. The Justices ordered a prisoner pleading clergy and claimed by the Bishop to be delivered to the Bishop, but in order that it might be known in what cha-

---

[1] Bracton says (fo. 421 *a*) that a peremptory exception lies against anyone who is "surdus et mutus naturaliter."

[2] "Nota qun qauoit par son attourne gage la ley de noun somons en plee de terre vynt en propre persone et ne poait parler mes faire signes et il oit et entendist ceo qe homme lui dit.—Et STONORE lui dist Si vous volez faire la ley mettez vostre mayn sour le livere. Et il mist sa mayn et les paroles de la charge furent dites par COURT." Year Books, Easter, 13 Edward III, p. 177 (Rolls Series). "Nota qun homme muet en *Precipe quod reddat* gagea sa ley de noun somons par signes autre frith et ore par signes fit la ley et les paroles luy furent reherces et il oyst et mist sa meyn outre le livere et le beisa et issint saunz parole parforny la ley." Mich. 18 Edward III, p. 291 (Rolls Series).

racter he was to be delivered they ordered an inquest by the country of the facts alleged against him. If the twelve jurors and the four neighbouring townships said upon their oath that he was guilty, he was delivered to the Bishop as guilty; if they said that he was not guilty, he was delivered as not guilty. You will note that this was not a trial. The indicted clerk has not submitted himself to it; he has not pleaded either guilty or not guilty; but a verdict has been taken. If it be a favourable one, the accused man is acquitted so far as a lay court can acquit him; if it be against him, then he is delivered to the Bishop for trial in the Bishop's Court. Of what happened there our records tell us little or nothing, but one gathers that the old process of compurgation was in use there, a process which enabled a criminal to clear himself with something like scandalous ease. This privilege was not confined to clerks in orders. The monks shared it with them; whether nuns might have claimed it, if they had unhappily stood in need of it, I do not know. There is no evidence either the one way or the other. There is in Fitz-herbert's *Abridgement*[1] a note that a woman, who was a clerk, was found guilty and was claimed by the Ordinary as a member of the Church. I do not quite understand in what sense a woman could be a "clerk," but if she could be properly entitled to be so designated then I see no reason why she should not be entitled to plead clergy. Of course, the lay court would not accept a prisoner's unsupported statement that he was a clerk. They required some proof of it. This was usually, in claims made *bona fide*, supplied by some reputable ecclesiastic. But if none such were present, none, at any rate, whose mere word the Court was inclined to accept, then the Court would inquire of three matters. Was the accused man dressed after the usual fashion of a clerk? Did his head show the tonsure? Could he read? Should a man fail in the second test he would, perhaps, explain that he had been in prison awaiting trial so long that his hair

---

[1] *Corone*, case 461 (22 Edward III). Hale (*Pleas of the Crown*, II, p. 327) says: "certainly by the Canon laws Nuns had the exemption from temporal juris- diction, but the privilege of clergy was never allowed them by our law"; but on p. 371 he says: "Anciently nuns professed were admitted to the privilege of clergy." For the full discussion of the subject of clergy, "which I [*sc.* Hale] must needs say is one of the most involved and difficult titles in the law," Chap. XLIV of the *Pleas of the Crown* may be read with much profit.

had grown and obliterated the tonsure. Sometimes a clerk, strong in the consciousness of provable innocence, would waive his clergy and put himself on the country. Such a course, if a favourable verdict was returned, resulted in his immediate acquittal. If he had insisted on his clergy he would have been delivered to the Bishop[1].

Let me reproduce for you in this connexion two scenes in the King's Bench in the Michaelmas Term of the twentieth year of Edward II, a year of which, and the fact is worth noting, the black-letter volume of 1678 knows nothing[2]. A man is arraigned for felony. He pleads clergy and claims to be tried by his Ordinary, but there is no ecclesiastic present to claim him as a clerk. It is pointed out to him that he is dressed in cloth of ray[3], which was not the usual vesture of clerks. He is asked how he explains this incongruity. He has, apparently, no explanation to give. Then the prosecuting Serjeant questions him in French and Latin. He understands neither language. He is now told to bend down his head. No tonsure is to be seen. He has failed in every test, and his claim is rejected. Much about the same time one William of Burton was arraigned in the same Court for a series of crimes. He was charged with having broken into a church and robbed it, with having broken out of the Marshalsea prison, and with some other serious offences. It may be noted here parenthetically that if a clerk robbed the Church he thereby, as a traitor to the Church, forfeited his right to the Church's protection. William pleaded his clergy and said that he ought not to plead before any judge except his own Ordinary. "The devil is your Ordinary," the Chief Justice said, and told him to show his head. William's head did show the tonsure, and he was able to read a book which was given into

[1] In the Eyre of Kent of 1313–14 Thomas of Sarre was charged with having poisoned his father. Being asked how he would acquit himself, he said that he was a clerk, but that, while saving his clergy, he put himself on the country. The Ordinary handed him a book and he read two verses therein. Spigurnel J. asked him: "Will you hold by your clergy or go to the jury? You must make your election of one or the other, for you cannot have both." Thomas put himself on the jury, who acquitted him. *Year Book Series* (Selden Society), v, p. 151.

[2] My authority is Hale MS. (Lincoln's Inn), 137 (2), fo. 239 d.

[3] The authorities seem to be at issue as to what "cloth of ray" actually was. On this see the Glossary at the end of *Bills in Eyre* (Selden Society, xxx), *s.v.*

his hands. So the Court had some doubt, and trouble lay ahead of the lay judge who irregularly dealt with an ordained clerk. Still if William had committed sacrilege, as was alleged, he had lost the Church's protection and might properly be dealt with by the lay court. This showed a way out of the difficulty. William was put back for the time, and the Chief Justice ordered a jury to be impanelled to try the question of fact whether William had in fact committed sacrilege. If that jury should find that he had, then William would lose any privilege he might otherwise have had. What conclusion that jury came to and what in the end happened to William is not chronicled[1]. It sometimes happened,

---

[1] I append the actual text of these interesting cases from the Lincoln's Inn MS.:

"Un Henry Lamberd fust areigne en baunke le Roy de ceo qil fut conuict laroun qe dit qil fut Clerk.

Scrope. Vous estes vestu des draps de Ray et cest a trauers par quei volez vous altre chose dire.

Henry. Ieo ne puisse mye respoundre sanz mes ordineres.

Scrope ly opposa en lateyn et en franceys et il ne sauoit mie respoundre et pus vint vn Moigne Labbe de Westmonastere et ly chalengea cum clerk.

Scrope. Abessez la teste et sic fecit et nauoit pas tonsure et les ordineres ne sount pas icy de vous chalenger com membre etc. et pus *Scrope* ad Monachum si vous ly chalengez come clerk et il ne seit pas clerk vous auerez la penaunce gensuwist qest tiele qe touz les temporaltez labbe en mesme leuesche seront forfaitz au Roy et qil perde cela fraunchise de chalenger clerk de ly et ses successours a touz iours.

Ordinere. Sil soit clerk nous le chalengoms et le liure de assayer sil sache lire.

Scrope. Nanyl ceo ne froms par deuant qe vous leyez chalenge et pus *Lordinere* wayua son chalenge et *Scrope* ly demanda direchief coment il se voleyt acquiter.

Henry. Ieo seu clerk.

Scrope rehercea com deuant coment il fut trouve en robe de Ray et ceo a trauers et coment il nauoit pas tonsure ne qil ne sauoit nen latyn nen fraunceys respoundre ne abit de clerk auoit par quei par ley de la Corone vous serrez mys a vostre penaunce ore est la ley si corteyse qe homme vous dirra quelle la penaunce est et serra deuant ceo qe vous soiez aiuge qe vous soyez mys en vne mesoun bien balaye et soyez vestu de vostre brays et chemyse sanz plus et qe vous portez tant de fer com vous poez porter et plus et qe vous eyez a manger du pyr pain qe homme purra troner et de ceo ne mye assez et qe vous beuez de lewe plus pres esteant de la prisoun a ceo iour qe vous mangez vous ne beuerez pas nec econtra par quei arrivez vous si vous volez mettre en pays qar si la penaunce vous soit enioynt mes qe vous vodrez pus mettre vous nauendrez pas.

Henry ne voleyt altre chose dire.

Scrope agarda qil fut mys a sa penaunce vt supra Et ita factum fuit."

"William de Burtone fut aregne en Baunk le Roy de ceo qil dust tratorousement auer pris le chastel de Walyngforde et qil dust auer bruse la prisoun del

as it actually happened in the first of the two cases to which reference has just been made, that these claimants to the privilege of clergy clove to it after it had been rejected by the Court and refused to plead before a lay judge. To such the same terrible punishment was meted as awaited the ordinary layman who for one reason or another refused to plead. The gaoler was ordered to strip him of all his clothes save some scrap of underclothing and to take him into a bare cell, without even a litter of straw on the floor, and there to lay upon him as great a weight of iron as he could support without having life straightway crushed out of him; to give him a bit of coarse bread to eat every other day, and, on the days when he had naught to eat, to give him a drink of water out of the nearest puddle, and so to continue till the man died. Nor was a subsequent repentance of his obstinacy and a willingness to plead of any avail. He had made his election once for all, and must abide by it to the end[1].

You will get, as you sit in these mediaeval Courts, occasional glimpses of happenings in our early Parliaments; sometimes of very dramatic happenings, scenes which are reported nowhere else. We may, for instance, see Edward I presiding over its deliberations, while he grows restless and weary of the arid technicalities of the Justices discussing what was the proper writ to serve on behalf of the King in certain circumstances. At last the King, who, the scribe of the book tells us, was passing wise, lost patience; and rising from his seat said to the Justices: "Naught wot I of your quibbling, but by God's blood you shall give me a good writ before you go hence[2]." From a Year Book of Henry VI we learn that a regular procedure had been formu-

Marchalcie et qil dust auer debruse leglise de sancto ketone (*sic*) et al tut il respoundist clericus sum et non debeo respondere nisi coram Indice meo ordinario nec alibi debeo convenire.

Scrope. Le diable est vostre iuge ordinere et pus *Scrope* dit Monstrez la teste et il auoit corone et lust en vn liure.

Scrope. Si nous eussoms par record ceo qe nous auoms par enditement nous ferroms bien de la clergie et pus dit il al attourne le Roy siwe iij. brefs a les visnets on il suppose les felonies estre festes de fere venir bon pays et pus dit qe si par enqueste doffice troue soit la debrusure del eglise ou la tresoun qil nenioyera mye sa clergie einz serra areigne et sil ne [*sic*] se mette bien est et si ceo noun il serra maunde a sa penaunce vt supra."

[1] See the case of H. Lamberd in the footnote on the preceding page, and *The Eyre of Kent* (Selden Society), I, pp. l, li.

[2] *Year Books* (Selden Society), III, p. 196 (3 Edward II).

lated in the respective cases of the Peers amending or not amending bills sent to them by the Commons, and in the further case of the Commons not accepting the Peers' amendments; and that it was already the settled practice that every bill should have reference to the first day of the Parliament in which it was introduced, even though, as a matter of fact, it was introduced at the end of the Parliament[1]. You may be present in Court when Chief Justice Hengham tells how Parliament has been making rules for the Court's procedure[2]; and you will hear of the tax-collectors being busily at work assessing the definite quota to be paid by each town of the taxes granted by Parliament.

To turn to other matters. We shall see in our mediaeval Courts customs which we still see used to-day. We shall see the Justices assigning counsel where they thought such a course desirable in the interests of justice. We shall see, certainly as far back as the thirty-fifth year of Edward I, the intervention of the *amicus curiae*, when Serjeant Willoughby, who is described as *non existens cum aliquo parcium*, rose in his place and advised the Court out of his experience[3]. But counsel actually engaged in arguing a case seem in the days of which the Year Books tell us to have been able to cast aside for a moment the part of active counsel and assume that of *amicus curiae*, and by this change of character found it possible to make objections which they would not have been allowed to make as counsel. Serjeant Markham, for instance, in 19 Henry VI, wanted to take exception to a certain count, but as he proposed to do so after, instead of before, taking exception to the writ, the Court, supporting the objection of the Serjeant on the other side, refused to allow him to do so. Markham thereupon said that the facts disclosed in the count were not sufficient in law to warrant the plaintiff's action, and though he might not be allowed to make the exception as counsel it was open to him to do so as *amicus curiae*, as it was open to any stranger to the case to do. And apparently he was allowed to do so[4]. There is what seems a strange little incident

---

[1] Easter, 33 Henry VI, p. 17, case 8.

[2] 32–33 Edward I, p. 429 (Rolls Series).

[3] 33–35 Edward I, p. 477 (Rolls Series).

[4] "Debte sur une obligacion. *Markam* demanda Iugement de brief pur certein cause et le brief quant a ceo fuit agarde bon et puis il voulait aver

chronicled in one of the Year Books of Henry VI, which could not very well occur to-day. In open Court Serjeant Yelverton offered Serjeant Markham forty pence if he would demur with him on a certain point of law. Markham was quite willing to accept the offer, but his client would not agree to his doing so[1]. Would the forty pence have gone to the client?

We hear in the earlier books, as we do not hear to-day, the Justices speaking of the Serjeants and the Serjeants speaking of each other by their Christian or baptismal names. But for our mediaeval ancestors this Christian name was the only real name. The surname, as the word itself implies, was a mere addition to the real name, added for purposes of differentiation. And you could not in those days have two names, that was more than once formally ruled by the Court, though you might have two or more surnames, and those at the same time[2]. When our mediaeval Justices said that a man could not have two baptismal names I do not think that they were declaring that a man might not receive two names at baptism, *e.g.* that he could not be baptised as William Henry, though no child was so doubly baptised, if the phrase may pass, in those days, but that whatever name had been given to him in baptism he must abide by it, with one exception of which I will treat presently. He could not vary it or duplicate it as he could vary or duplicate his surname. But there was a recognised exception to this rule. A man or woman might change his or her name at Confirmation.

---

demander Iugement de Connt. A qei *Hody.* A ceo ne serez recens entant qe avez demande Iugement de brief purqei vous avez passez le pas. Purqei le *Court* dit a *Markam.* Vous naurez cest excepcion *causa qua supra. Markam.* Cest excepcion est matiere aparannte en le connt qe nest pas suffisaunte en *Ley* purqei nous purroms aver cest excepcion come *Amicus Curiae* et issint peut le plus estranger de monde de matiere qui appert." Year Books, Mich. 19 Henry VI, p. 10, case 26. See also Hil. 4 Henry VI, p. 16, case 16, and Tr. 16 Henry VII, p. 11, case 5.

[1] Mich. 20 Henry VI, p. 4, case 12.

[2] "Homme ne puit auer ij. nosmes de baptisme mes homme poet bien auer ij. surnosmes et estre conus per lun et lautre." Year Books, 9 Edward IV, p. 43; and see Mich. 21 Edward IV, p. 56, line 10.

"*Mutford.* Yl y ad meynt home ky ad deus surnonns ansi cum Sire Roger le fyz Osebern et Sire Roger le fiz Peres et par amedeus est yl conuz." 21–22 Edward I, p. 333 (Rolls Series).

"*Bereford.* Il est possible qe un homme eit diuers surnons." Additional Manuscript 35116 (British Museum), *temp.* Edward II, fo. 73 *d.*

"It may be," Chief Justice Bereford said in 5 Edward II of a woman whose name was in dispute, "that she was christened Denise and afterwards received the name Alice in Confirmation, or *vice versa*, and the name which the Bishop gave her will be her right name[1]." And what the mediaeval Justices declared to be the law in their time remains, I believe, the law to-day. I do not know of any legal way of changing the baptismal name after Confirmation. The custom of giving two or more names in baptism is comparatively modern. More than once I have detected a corruption in Year Book manuscripts, corruptions which I might not otherwise have suspected, by finding some one apparently in the possession of a double Christian name.

Then, again, we hear of legal theories of which we hear no more to-day. The Church, the mediaeval lawyers said, was always under age[2], and could claim all the advantages of infancy. This was always allowed without objection. Once or twice a Serjeant tried to set up a similar theory as to the King—that the King was always under age. But this theory did not succeed in getting itself established, the Court showing what inequitable consequences would necessarily follow from such a theory if it were allowed[3]. The theories that the King can do no wrong[4] and that time does not run against him[5] go very far back, so that he need not complain overmuch if legal theory has refused to confine him in a constitutional nursery all the days of his life. Amongst other privileges of the King was his immunity from being vouched to warranty[6].

Scraps of contemporary history are preserved for us in these old books which historians have not recorded. We learn, for

[1] *Year Book Series* (Selden Society), XI, p. 153. On this see also I Inst. cap. 1, Sect. 1, quoting Herle in 9 Edward III; and for some modern instances see Phillimore's *Ecclesiastical Law* (2nd edit.), 1, p. 518, and *Jones v. E. Hulton and Co.* L.R. [1909], 2 K.B. p. 451.

[2] See, *e.g.* 21 Edward I, p. 32; 33 Edward I, p. 453 (Rolls Series); and also Inst. II, cap. 1, p. 3, citing Glanvill, Bracton and other authorities.

[3] 34 Edward I, p. 230 (Rolls Series). "*Bereford.* Si le Roy fut tut temps denz age nul qil facit lui liereit a vostre dit cuius contrarium est verum." Lincoln's Inn MS. 139, fo. 144 *d.*

[4] See Year Books, 1 Richard III, p. 8, case 13.

[5] 34 Edward I, p. 230 (Rolls Series).

[6] 21–22 Edward I, p. 287 (Rolls Series).

instance, how when Edward II went to Burton-on-Trent with
his army to fight the rebels he had encamped with him a great
number of Frenchmen, and how these Frenchmen, for some un-
recorded reason, sallied out and massacred the villeins of the
manor and did much other general damage[1]. What actually
happened when an action was set down for hearing in the
country between litigants who could bring troops of retainers
into Court a report of 7 Henry VI makes plain to us. Justices
went down to try an assize in Cumberland. It was promptly
adjourned to Westminster, and Babington C.J., who was one
of the Justices who had gone down to Cumberland, tells us why.
The issue, he said, was an important one, and the parties came
into Court with great crowds of armed retainers, more as though
they had come to fight a battle than to be present at an assize.
And because if the hearing had been continued in the country
the King's peace would probably have been broken, it was
therefore adjourned to Westminster[2]. We have, to pick out
almost at random another fragmentary chronicle, an interesting
story from the rebellion of Jack Cade. A number of blood-
thirsty scoundrels supporting him came into Bath with the
intention of beheading several of the leading citizens who were
opposed to the "haut et grand traytre," as the reporting scribe
calls him, unless their proposed victims were willing to redeem
their lives by a sufficient payment in cash. The story as the
Year Book tells it is that these rebels captured a certain loyalist,
whose name is not given us, and forcibly took him to the High
Cross and there attempted to cut off his head. Some friends of
the unhappy man, however, rallied to his rescue and hurried him
off for safety to the mayor's house, and begged the mayor to
keep him there all night lest he should be caught again and
murdered. The mayor promised to do so, and did so; and then
the ungrateful fellow brought an action for false imprisonment
against his rescuers. The report does not tell us the result of it,
but if the true facts were anything like those set out, I can only
hope that he not only lost it but was soundly amerced for his

[1] Year Books, Trin. 19 Edward II, p. 668.
[2] "Assize fuit arrame devant Sir *W. Babington* et *Strange* en le County de
Comberland et fuit adiorne devant eux memes a Westminstre. Et *Fulthorpe*

monstrous claim[1]. As a last matter of historical interest we may note that Chief Justice Hengham tells us that it was he who drafted the Statute of Westminster II[2].

We shall listen sometimes to interesting discussions on what we may perhaps call domestic economy, domestic discipline certainly, sometimes. Where, for instance, is it lawful for you to thrash your apprentice? I do not mean on what part of his body, but in what part of England. Can you do so only in the place where he was apprenticed to you, where your established workshop is, or may you thrash him elsewhere, at a fair, for instance, at which you have set up a temporary stall? Then, again, may you thrash him twice or oftener for the same offence? These questions were discussed in a case that was tried in 21 Edward IV. The defendant had gone, from London probably, with his apprentice to the great fair on Barnwell Common, just outside Cambridge, and had set up a stall there. Seemingly the apprentice had refused to sell his master's wares, and his master had thereupon given him a thrashing; and, apparently,

demanda des Iustices la cause dil adiornement etc. *Babington* dit pur ceo qe il est grand matter et les parties en lour propre Counties viendrent ore grand routes des gens darmes plus semble a venir a battaile qe al Assise et issint pur doubtes qe la paix le Roy serroit distourbe et auxi pur ceo qe cy a Londres fuit le conseil et les parties icy puissent estre servis de lour droit: pur ceo nous adiornames l'assise." Year Books, 7 Henry VI, p. 9, case 15.

[1] "Brief de Faux imprisonment fuit porte envers divers persones. Le pleintif suppose per son brief qe les defendants luy assauterent, baterent et emprisonerent tanque il pur son deliverance fist fine etc. Et les defendants disoient qe action etc. car ils disoient qe en le temps de insurrection et rebellion de Jack Cade le haut et grande traytre etc. un W. Skinner de Bathe etc. assemble oue luy divers malefactors al nombre de persons [*sic*] et plusors, les queux malefactors assenterent et accorderent perenter eux et de ceux qe furent notables gens il veulent oppresser sinon qe ils veulent faire fine oue eux et de ceux queux il haint ils veulent couper les testes et dient oustre qe les dits malefactors tiel iour etc. vindrent en la dit ville de Bathe et la prindrent ove force et armes le dit pleintif et luy amesnerent al Haut crosse de mesme la ville et la veulent aver coupe son teste, et les dits defendants voiants le mischief et inconvenience qe purreit de ceo ensuir vindrent ove autres al dit pleintif et mit sur luy lour mains peasiblement et luy prindrent et amesnerent al meason dun J. B. adonque Mayor del dit ville et la prierent le dit Mayor qe le dit [pleintif] purreit estre en sa meason pur tout le nuit adonque ensuant en saufguard de sa vie, per force de quel il fuit la herberge etc. le quel est mesme l'enprisonment, assaut et batery dont le pleintif ad conceu sa action; le quel matter etc. Et quant al fine ils disent qe se ne fist ascun fine." Year Books, Hil. 35 Henry VI, p. 44, case 6.

[2] Mich. 33 Edward I, p. 83 (Rolls Series). "HENGHAM. Ne glosez point le statut nous le sauoms meuz de vous qar nous le feimes."

had repeated that thrashing later on to ensure the apprentice's remembering it. The apprentice's counsel argued that a master might thrash his apprentice only at home, and that the thrashing could not be repeated. But Fairfax J. disagreed. He held that you might thrash your apprentice anywhere where he disobeyed your lawful commands; and you might quite properly say to such a disobedient apprentice, "For your disobedience you have deserved six stripes. I shall give you two to-day, two to-morrow and two the next day"; but *semble* that you could not thrash him twice for the same offence unless you had at the outset given him notice that his adjudged punishment was going to be meted out to him on the instalment principle[1].

All these things of which I have told you, and many another, were being noted in some sort of mediaeval stenography by a company of reporters. Who or how many these reporters were I cannot with any certainty tell you. Possibly, even probably, they were apprentices of the law. Possibly, and again probably, they took these notes in that "crib" which was provided for their use. What these reporters hurriedly jotted down with their pens as their ears followed the ceaseless flow of speech, arguments *pro* and *con*, repartees, jibes, stories and what not, somewhat expanded, probably, in the quiet of the afternoon or evening while the recollection of it all was fresh in the mind, make up what we call the Year Books, or the greater portion of them. These books are for the most part written in dialogue form in the Anglo-Norman of the time. They are by far the earliest reports of things actually said, in the very words in which they were said. There is nothing else like them anywhere. They are a unique source of information as to the Anglo-Norman language spoken in England in the Middle Age, not the con-

---

[1] "*Spilm.* Il appert icy qe le defendant battit le pleintiff en autre ville hors de L. et ieo entende qe homme ne poit battre son apprentice en autre ville mes lou il est fait apprentice et auxy il ne poit luy battre 2 foits pur un meme cause. *Fairfax.* Ceo nest issint car sil ale al faire a Cambridge pur vendre son merchandise et il commande son apprentice de vendre son chaffere et il refuse nest il loyal pur luy battre. Ieo die qe cy. Et qant a lautre case de battre luy 2 foits pur un cause il est loyal car sil dit al apprentice vous auez deserve 6 stripes pur cet defaute et vous avez 2 cet iour et 2 lendemain etc. ascun disereit donqes il serra batti infinite pur un cause qil nest reason." Year Books, Mich. 21 Edward IV, p. 53, case 17.

sidered and more or less artificial and unreal speech of the study, of the dramatist or poet, but the actual words taken from the mouths of the actual speakers, the actual words as they were born of the feeling of the moment. They give us, too, many a scrap of our old English tongue. They tell us much of the trades and businesses in which mediaeval men and women in England were engaged. In them are preserved the names of trades and callings which have so long fallen into desuetude that not even all the philological learning of Professor Skeat could satisfy him of the meaning. One may sum it all up by saying that there are few questions about mediaeval life in England and the conditions in which it was lived which the Year Books, intelligently questioned, will not answer; and even what I have told you so briefly and incompletely of their contents is enough to justify Maitland's statement that "it will some day seem a wonderful thing that men once thought that they could write the history of mediaeval England without using the Year Books.... The Year Books come to us from life. Some day they will return to life again at the touch of some great historian[1]."

Consider the Year Books for a moment from another point of view; one which will still further emphasize their value. The common law of England is the common law of the United States of America. That is a fact which here I need do no more than barely state. England's system of common law was England's great gift to America. No one more frankly allows that than do American lawyers. As recently as September, 1922, Judge Clearwater, formerly a Justice of the Supreme Court of New York and lately President of the New York Bar Association, wrote in the London *Spectator*:

From the beginning and to this day our lawyers, judges and Courts of Justice undeviatingly have been unstinted in acknowledging the great debt of our people to the Common Law of England....We regard it as flexible and as always adapted to meet new and unexpected cases. Its fundamental principles we treat as immutable[2].

[1] *Year Book Series* (Selden Society), I, p. xx.
[2] "The common law is the basis of the laws of every State and Territory of the Union, with comparatively unimportant and gradually waning exceptions." J. F. Dillon, *Laws and Jurisprudence of England and America* (1894), p. 155.

Lord Bacon has told us that the Common Law of England is no text law, "but the substance of it consisteth in the series and succession of Judicial Acts from time to time which have been set out in the books which we term Year Books[1]." The common law of America is, therefore, set out in the Year Books. The immigrant into America, no matter whence he comes, lives a law which is fundamentally English law. Our common fundamental Common Law, England's common law and America's common law, is set out by our common ancestors in books which belong to the common national literature of England and America. Yet it is the knowledge of the contents of documents like these, so many-sided in their value, as I have tried to show you, which the apathy of England, her neglect of one of her greatest literary treasures, the like of which no other nation possesses, allowed to wither away. Instead of being the common property of every man and woman of culture, they became the secret hoard of a few legal scholars. "They should have been our glory," Maitland said, "they are our disgrace, for no other nation would have so neglected them[2]."

[1] "A Memorial touching the Review of Penal Laws and the Amendment of the Common Law." *The Letters and Life of Francis Bacon* (ed. Jas. Spedding, 1869), v, p. 85.

[2] *History of English Law* (Pollock and Maitland), I, p. xxxv (2nd edit.).

II

THE YEAR BOOKS IN MANUSCRIPT: THEIR BIRTH-PLACE AND AUTHORS: THEIR EVOLUTION

I GAVE, in my first lecture, some very general pictures of the Court of Common Bench in which, for the most part, the early reports of our Year Books were made. I want now to give a more detailed account of the surroundings of that Court, of the circumstances in which our mediaeval reporters did their work. Let us get back to Westminster Hall five, six or seven hundred years ago. In 1224 Henry III ordained three judgment seats in the Hall; at the entry, on the right hand, the Court of Common Bench or Common Pleas; at the upper end of the Hall, on the right hand, in the south-east corner, the King's Bench; on the left hand or south-west corner, the Chancery. I have already ventured upon some sort of rough computation of the number of people who were in actual attendance upon the Court of Common Bench. Perhaps we may get some hint of it from a remark addressed by Sir William Bereford, the Chief Justice of that Court, in Edward II's reign. "There are forty fools here," he said, "who think," well, to put it shortly, nonsense. I am not going to pin labels on to the forty fools, but I suppose that Bereford meant the expression to cover those, at any rate, who ought to have known better, the Serjeants and apprentices. However many there may have been in attendance upon the Court of Common Bench, it is probable that there were something like as many in attendance upon each of the other Courts; added to, in the case of the King's Bench, if we may trust the old illumination to which I have already made reference, by a string of rather terrible looking prisoners, some of them half naked, some of them manacled. After all, Westminster Hall is not a very vast place, and if there had been naught and no one else there than these three Courts and those who were in one capacity or another in attendance upon them, there must, one thinks, have been a good deal of noise and confusion, hardly compatible with the clear hearing by the reporters of the speeches

and interjected remarks of Justices and Counsel. But there were
other sources of noise and confusion besides these. There were
stalls of merchandises in the Hall. What these merchandises were
I do not know; possibly what we nowadays call refreshments;
possibly and very probably, I think, pens, ink and parchment.
At a much later period it is said that pamphlets were sold in the
Hall. In 18 Edward IV Bryan C.J.C.B., discussing the validity
of a contract for sale, said: "Suppose that I sell you all the caps
and hats in Westminster Hall[1]." It is arguable that he was
speaking of caps and hats exposed for sale in the Hall. Certainly
if to-day anyone spoke of contracting to sell all the hats and
costumes in Bond Street, he would be taken to refer to those
exposed for sale in the shops and not to those in actual use by
passers to and fro in the street. But I feel uncertain, in lack of
other evidence, as to what Bryan C.J. exactly meant. Still his
remark does point to the possibility of Westminster Hall being
a sort of bazaar for the sale of all sorts of goods. And, as I do
not know certainly what was sold at these stalls, neither do I
know how many of these stalls there were; but that there were
a good many of them, served by a good many people, seems plain
from the report of a case in Edward III's reign. A woman who
was plaintiff in an action was attacked in Court by her opponent,
a man, who beat and maltreated her. The Court ordered a jury
of the people of the stalls of merchandises—*les gentz des stalles
des marchandises*—to be sworn immediately to try the assault[2].
The working theory of a jury in those days, you will remember,
was that it was a body of men who knew the facts of the matter
of their own knowledge, and had not to depend, as a jury has to
depend to-day, upon the evidence of other people, knowing
nothing about the matter themselves. If twelve men could be
withdrawn from these stalls in Westminster Hall without
leaving them unattended and unprotected, and I think that we
may assume that they would not be so left, the staff must have
been a fairly numerous one, and the stalls fairly numerous too.

[1] "*Brian*. Si ieo vende a vous touts les bonets et hatts que sont en le sale
de Westmoustre." Year Books, 18 Edward IV, p. 20, case 29.
[2] "Sur ceo Knivet Justice commanda Marsh' de faire un Panel meintenant
des gens qe auent stalles de marchandise en mesme la sale." *Liber Assisarum*,
47 Edward III, p. 261, case 18.

But not yet have we exhausted all the possible sources of noise and disturbance. Somewhere underneath the Bench, *sub banco*, was a place called "Hell," *quidam locus qui vocatur Helle*. We do not know very much about this Hell, but it does not seem to have been an over-restful place. It is described as being "hic in aula sub banco." This *hic in aula* seems to show that it was some sort of a cellar or vault opening immediately into the Hall, and the only record of it that I know speaks of an assault that was committed there[1]. The fact I want to bring home to you is this. Westminster Hall, when the Courts were sitting, must have been little short of a Babel. You have the three, or rather four Courts[2], each with its concomitant crowd of Serjeants, apprentices, clerks, attorneys, litigants, jurors, with prisoners and gaolers, too, in the case of the King's Bench, and I know not who else besides. You have I know not how many stalls selling something, with the dealers and their customers chaffering with each other; you may have, apparently, people who are not over orderly emerging from time to time from a vault in close contiguity to the Bench; you have, one gathers, as many of the outside public as chose to come in, strolling about from Court to Court and from stall to stall, for there were no seats where they could quietly bestow themselves under the eyes of order-keeping ushers, making, we cannot doubt, their own private comments to their immediate neighbours. Every now and again there seems to have been something like an open riot in the Hall, when one of the greater of the King's subjects was party to an action and came attended by a retinue of his people and took objection to the course of the proceedings. Every now and again there were more or less savage assaults made by parties to actions upon each other; and sometimes the very officers of the Courts quarrelled and fought amongst themselves. This was the setting in which the High Courts of the Realm administered justice some centuries ago. These were the surroundings in which the men who gave us what, with some subsequent

[1] De Banco Plea Roll, Hil. 3 Edward II (No. 180), r. 69. For the "houses or mansions," contiguous to the Hall, called "Paradise," "Hell" and "Purgatory," see *Calendar of Patent Rolls*, 1547–1548, p. 248.

[2] *i.e.* the King's Bench, two divisions of the Common Bench, and the Chancery.

expansion, perhaps, made in circumstances of less pressure and in greater quietness, became our Year Books, or a great part of them, that great part of them which reports the proceedings in actions tried in Westminster Hall. But besides the Year Books containing reports of these proceedings at Westminster, for the most part of actions tried in the Common Bench, we have many others which for the sake of convenience we also call Year Books, because their contents are of a like nature, though the term is not, perhaps, strictly correct—the Year Books of the Eyres. At varying intervals, supposed never to be less than seven years, from Henry II's time to the tenth year of Edward III, commissions of Justices were sent by the King into the several counties to try all manner of pleas arising therein. I must not here go into any detailed account of these Courts of Eyre. It must suffice here to say that they were vested with all the powers inherent in the King. They administered both law and equity. The King's residual or extraordinary function of causing justice to be done where ordinary means failed lay in their hands, and they were not only entitled but bound to exercise it. And the Year Books of the Eyres have, further, this special importance. In 1289, just the date of our earliest surviving Year Book of terms at Westminster, the trial of writs of *quo warranto* was withdrawn from the jurisdiction of the Courts at Westminster and assigned exclusively to the Justices of the General Eyres. Consequently it is in the Year Books of the Eyres alone that any reports of the trial of those writs during the years in which they were most freely used for the protection of the King's rights and, incidentally, for the replenishment of his Exchequer, abounding, as they do, in instruction as to the franchises and privileges of many ancient manors, have come down to us.

Besides reports of all the varied judicial proceedings in Eyre the Year Books of the Eyres give us the full story of all the preliminary work in preparation of an Eyre which had to be done by the Sheriffs and Coroners and other officials of the county, details of all the ceremonies observed when the commission was opened, of the many and various proclamations issued by the Justices before they betook themselves to their judicial duties, stories of the searching of taverns for musty wine and ale, of the assessing of the prices for which food might be sold while the Eyre was in session, a matter which sometimes gave rise to a good deal of trouble, for purchasers and vendors do not always find themselves in strict accord as to what are fair selling values[1]. The process by bills in Eyre was a remarkable process peculiar to the Eyres. I must not go into that most interesting procedure now, but must content myself with just saying that we owe to the reports in the Year Books of its application and working many interesting details of mediaeval life in England. One of the minor facts one gathers from these Year Books, though it is nowhere specifically stated, is that, as in the Common Bench at Westminster, so in the Common Pleas division, at any rate, of the Eyres, right of audience was restricted to the Serjeants. We find the same Serjeants, and Serjeants only, pleading in Eyre as we find pleading at Westminster. It must be added to this story of the contents of the Year Books, that a certain number of reports of assizes, heard in the country before Justices specially assigned to try them, has been preserved in true Year Book form.

We are not dependent for the reports of any particular year or term upon one manuscript or book alone. For most of the terms many manuscripts survive, of the relationship of which to one another I will say something presently. Take, for instance, as fairly typical, the first seven years of Edward II. Seventeen manuscripts at least survive which give reports of actions tried in those years or in some of them. Of these seventeen manuscripts four are in the Cambridge University Library, one in the Bodleian at Oxford, ten in the British Museum and two in the Library of Lincoln's Inn. I shall not give you a detailed description of all these seventeen manuscripts, and I might weary you if I attempted one; but I may very properly say something definite and detailed about the four manuscripts in the Cambridge University Library. The first of these manuscripts of which I will speak has for its press-mark Ff. 3. 12. It bears the name of Henri de Motelow on the recto of folio 111 and on the verso of folio 113, and we may presume that he was the owner of the manuscript. He was appointed a Justice of the Common Bench on 4 July, 1357, and as no fines were levied

---

[1] *The General Eyre*, pp. 27–29 and 41.

before him after Easter, 1361, he probably died a little later.
This manuscript then, which contains reports up to the last
year of Edward II, must have come into his possession not many
years after it was written. On the recto of folio 149 is written
"Basset est magister huius libri ut dicit Armiston," and Basset's
name is written again later on in a margin. I cannot with any
certainty identify either Basset or Armiston, but the writing
seems not likely to be later than sometime in Edward III's reign.
But here, once for all, I must warn you of the danger of trying
to date a manuscript from the nature of the writing. That has
been very sufficiently shown to us in recent years by Mr Hilary
Jenkinson. The precise date of a manuscript, if we have nothing
more to guide us than the character of the script, can never be
more than a matter of conjecture. This manuscript which I
am describing contains on its first nineteen folios reports of the
Eyre of Kent of 1313, 5 Edward II. Then follow reports of the
Common Bench of the first four years of Edward II. Then
there is a gap in the reports, until the tenth year, when the series
goes on regularly to the end of the reign. It would seem probable that the gap between the reports of the fourth and tenth
years is not due to any loss of folios, but that the reports of the
missing years were never included in the Collection. Gg. 5. 20
is the press-mark of the second Cambridge manuscript to which
I will refer. Two or three quires have seemingly been lost from
the earlier part of the book. It contains at present continuous
reports from the Hilary term of the second year to the end of the
Michaelmas term of the seventh year of Edward II. Then there is
a gap until the Michaelmas Term of the tenth year, from which
term the reports continue without a break, with one or two small
exceptions, until the end of the Trinity term of the eighteenth
year. The only clue as to its early ownership is given us by the
name Tremayne, written on the recto of folio 30. There was a
Serjeant of that name who practised in the latter part of Edward
III's reign. Possibly, one might say probably, I think, it was
Serjeant Tremaine who once owned this manuscript, which I
may add is beautifully written and more accurate than most of
our manuscripts. A third Cambridge manuscript which has for
its press-mark Ff. 2. 12 does not call for any long notice. It is

probably of somewhat later date than most of the other manuscripts giving us reports of the reign of Edward II. The first
eight folios are missing, and also those which were originally
numbered 90 and 101. With these exceptions the manuscript
is in a good condition. The first surviving folio begins in the
middle of the last case reported as of the Hilary term of
2 Edward II, and then we have a full series of reports which are
continuous until the end of the Trinity term of the eighteenth
year. No early owner has jotted down anything which will
enable us to identify him; but we do know that it once belonged
to John Moore who was Bishop of Norwich from 1691 to 1707,
and then of Ely until his death in 1714 when his Collection of
books and manuscripts was bought by George I and given by him
to Cambridge University. The last of the Cambridge manuscripts
—catalogued as Dd. 9. 64—is, in its present condition, the least
helpful of the four. It has been much damaged in places by
damp, and many of the reports cannot now be deciphered. It
contains a continuous series of reports from the Michaelmas
term of 2 Edward II to the Michaelmas term of the seventh
year, when it breaks off abruptly through the loss of the succeeding folios. There is nothing in it to indicate its previous owners.

Between the making in Court by somebody of the notes from
which the Year Books as we possess them now were evolved and
those actual Year Books themselves there lies a great gap. Can
we fill it up and say how the notes became the Year Books?
Only, I am afraid, conjecturally, by reasonably plausible theories.
But, before I go into that question, I ought to say something to
tell those who may not already know, what the Year Books, the
manuscript Year Books as we have them to-day, are like. And,
first, as to the period of time they cover. Where are we to find the
beginning of the Year Books? No short answer can be given to
that question. For one thing, it is certain that early manuscripts
which certainly once existed have now disappeared. The work
we know as Fitzherbert's *Abridgement* consists of a series of
extracts from Year Books arranged under headings of the various
subjects to which the extracts are apposite. It was first published
in 1514. Fitzherbert clearly had in his possession manuscript
Year Books which cannot now be traced, books of an earlier

date than any now known to exist. The oldest one was probably a book of the Wiltshire Eyre of 12 Edward I[1]. Closely rivalling this in age were a book of the Northamptonshire Eyre of the following year (13 Edward I) and a book of reports of cases heard at Westminster also in 13 Edward I. Fitzherbert has many references to each of these three books in his *Abridgement*[2]. Such books were clearly in his possession. He seems also to have had another book of reports of Edward I's time in which the cases were not certainly dated, and he does not venture to assign to the extracts which he makes from this book any more definite date than "en le temps Edward I." This evidence alone proves certainly that men were engaged in reporting cases as far back as 12 Edward I (1283–84). But the extracts from these reports which Fitzherbert has preserved for us are all that now remains to us of them. At any rate they have disappeared, though it does not necessarily follow that they do not still exist. They may be buried away somewhere in some old and unexplored library. But there is still certainly in existence a book of reports which seem to come from a considerably earlier time than the earliest books in Fitzherbert's possession. In Cambridge University Library is a manuscript volume[3] which contains, amongst other matter, nearly forty consecutive folios of reports of cases which can be dated only by the names of the Justices mentioned in them. Amongst these Justices are Preston and Seton and Littlebury. Gilbert of Preston was a Justice itinerant in 1240, and a Justice of the Common Bench in 1241 or perhaps

[1] For reasons why some extracts given by Fitzherbert and assigned by him to a still earlier date cannot be accepted as coming from true Year Book sources, see the Rolls Series of Year Books, 20 Edward III (2), p. l.

[2] It may be useful to give a list here of these early cases in Fitzherbert. From the Wiltshire Eyre of 12 Edward I he has: *Age*, case 130; *Assise*, 405; *Attaint*, 71; *Avowry*, 236; *Dower*, 3; *Garde*, 138; *Graunt*, 87. From the Northamptonshire Eyre of 13 Edward I he has: *Admesurement*, 17; *Age*, 155; *Assise*, 404; *Avowry*, 235; *Briefe*, 868; *Confirmation*, 19; *Dower*, 172; *Estoppel*, 272; *Garde*, 136, 137; *Linere*, 6; *Mesne*, 73; *Mordauncestre*, 47; *Par que Semicia*, 23; *Several tenauncy*, 4; *Villeinage*, 36, 44; *Voucher*, 269. To the book containing reports of cases heard at Westminster in 13 Edward I, Fitzherbert has the following references: *Attachement*, 8; *Bastardy*, 27; *Counterple de voucher*, 118; *Droit*, 31; *Enfant*, 16; *Formedon*, 63; *Villeinage*, 37, 38.

[3] The press-mark of this volume is Dd. 7. 14. For an interesting general account of its contents see Year Books of 20–21 Edward I (Rolls Series), pp. xi–xx.

earlier. Roger of Seton was a Justice of the Common Bench in 1268, and Martin of Littlebury is mentioned as a Justice of the King's Bench in 1272 (1 Edward I), but he had acted as a Justice taking assizes certainly as early as 1247 (31 Henry III)[1]. It does not seem too much to say that the contents of this volume are proof that probably as far back as the later years of Henry III men were taking notes in Court for subsequent expansion and transcription and that the first Year Books came into existence not later than that date. But it is not until we come to 20 Edward I that we have the commencement of a fairly consecutive series of Year Books actually known to be in existence; though, as we have seen, it is certain that there were books once in existence dating from a considerably earlier time. There are some terms of Edward I later than the twentieth year missing; several terms of Richard II and certainly one of Henry VI; and there are intermissions in the reigns of Henry VII and VIII. They stop finally in 1535, when their place was taken by reports made by counsel who printed and published them in their own names.

We have, as I have said, seventeen of these manuscripts giving us reports of actions tried in the earlier years of Edward II's reign. Not all of these, as you will have gathered, give reports relating to the same terms. Those which give reports of the same terms do not all give all the cases reported by one or other of them. Cases which are given by one manuscript may not be given by another. Where two or more manuscripts give reports of the same cases, the reports are not identical; but they are often so nearly identical that we cannot have the least doubt that the ultimate authority for them was one and the same. None of the manuscript Year Books now surviving can be looked upon as an original work. They are all copied, with, possibly, additions or omissions from pre-existing compilations of a like nature, which were probably copies themselves of still earlier compilations. What form the really original report took we must leave for later consideration. While some of our Year Books give us reports of particular cases in almost identical words, others will give us reports of the same cases in versions so different from

[1] Foss's *Judges of England*.

the first set that no collation with them is possible. In some cases we may get three or even more uncollatable versions. One reporter gives prominence to certain arguments and pleas, another to others; each noting what from his own point of view he thought most important. Then, again, the variant reports do not always seem all to have been taken at the same stage of the hearing of the action reported. And that raises a puzzling question which I will not now do more than just mention. When, at what particular stage of the hearing of an action, were the reports made? Though notes are frequent in them of something that was said or done "afterwards" or "on another day," the reports are always assigned to some particular term of a particular year. All the reporters do not always assign it to the same time, though they are not, as a rule, more than a term or two in disagreement. As a matter of fact many of the actions reported dragged their slow length along through several years; and, as I have just said, many of our reports give us the happening at more hearings than one. How was the particular date under which the report is given assigned? I can do no more to-day than just mention the matter. Sometimes the scribe of one of these compilations, of these manuscript Year Books, seems to have copied from one set of original sources, and sometimes from another. Some of the books resemble each other very closely in their contents, both in the reports given and in the actual form of those reports. Others differ widely in both respects. They are written, of course, in mediaeval book-script, some of them better and more easy of decipherment than others. The script abounds in abbreviations, and the text in omissions and repetitions and corruptions of one sort and another. A modern transcriber of them must have a long experience before he can feel a reasonable confidence in his reading of words and abbreviations here and there, or in his emendations of a scribe's guess at the word he was trying to copy but could not himself read. Let me quote you a few words, and I know how very true they are, from the most valuable work on *English Court Hand*, by Mr Charles Johnson and Mr Hilary Jenkinson; and Court Hand, I would have you note, does not contain quite so many pitfalls into which an unwary decipherer may fall as does the

Book Hand in various varieties of which the Year Books are written. This is what Mr Johnson and Mr Jenkinson say about some of the difficulties in deciphering the mediaeval Court Hand.

It will also be found that the very possibility of seeing what is actually written depends on the power of the reader to imagine for himself what ought to have been written and to check his hypotheses by what he can see. It is not too much to say that you cannot read a word with certainty unless you know what it is[1].

Who were the first authors or begetters of the terminal reports, of those books of terms as they were called in earlier days, which, when collected and copied in greater or less number, became what we have to-day, the manuscript Year Books? On the question of the first origin of the Year Books much has been written; and, according to the general judgment of present-day expert scholars, much of the ink used has been wasted. But probably the scholars of the future will have something of the same sort of criticism to make about our use of ink to-day. It is impossible to go into this question of the authorship of the original reports, which subsequently became, in the form of more or less extensive Collections, the books which we call the Year Books without repeating something of what modern scholars have written, something of what I have written myself. Still, in these lectures on the Year Books I ought not to slur over what is one of the most difficult questions concerning them too hurriedly. What, then, was the origin of the original reports made in the Courts at Westminster, in the Courts of the General Eyre, in the Courts of the Justices assigned to take assizes in the country? From the seventeenth century up to a comparatively recent time it was very generally believed and very dogmatically asserted that they had some sort of an official origin. Coke, Bacon and Blackstone all believed this, and said it; entertaining, apparently, not the least doubt about it. How came they to say this and to believe it so undoubtingly? It seems certain that this until recently generally accepted theory of the origin of the reports, which copied and re-copied and re-copied again and collected in terms and years became what we call

---

[1] *English Court Hand*, by Charles Johnson and Hilary Jenkinson (1915), Part I, p. xxxvii.

Year Books, rests ultimately upon some words written by Plowden in the Preface to his *Commentaries* or *Reports* first published in 1571. Before Plowden's time I do not know that anybody had thought the matter worth thinking about. What Plowden said was this:

> As I have heard on good authority there were four reporters of our law cases, who were men selected for the purpose, and who had an annual stipend for their labours in the matter paid by the King of this Kingdom, and they conferred together in drawing up and producing a report.

Blackstone embroiders and adds to Plowden's statement without showing any authority for his additions at all. He tells us that these reports were taken by the protonotaries or chief scribes of the Courts at the expense of the Crown, and published annually, whence they are called Year Books. As a matter of fact they were not called Year Books till a time long after the fourteenth century. When they were mentioned in Court they were simply "the books." They were not Year Books or books of years in their original form. They were at the most books of terms. It was not until many of these books of terms had been collected and copied and circulated as a whole that the name of Year Books was given to them. Coke merely echoed Plowden when he said somewhat pontifically and without the allegation of any authority that "it doth evidently appear that the Kings of this realm did select and appoint four discreet and learned professors of law to report the judgments and opinions of the reverend Judges." Bacon makes no specific statement on the matter, but only used the theory, which he plainly believed, as an argument for a new system of official reporting. I must not here even epitomize all that has been said and written by competent scholars in criticism of Plowden's statement. I must ask you to take it from me that Plowden's theory of the authorship of the Year Books is to-day discredited by all competent scholars. I think that I am justified in saying as much as that, yet one most competent scholar, Mr G. J. Turner, has made very able replies[1] to the several objections which have been taken to it, though I do not think that he would care to support it himself;

[1] Selden Society's *Year Book Series*, VI, ix–xix.

indeed, I have his personal authority for saying that he does not. Sir Frederick Pollock, the Literary Director of the Selden Society, has given this as his considered opinion: "I hold," he has written, "that the legend of the Year Books having had an official or even a semi-official character (which I tried to find credible so long as I could) is now finally exploded[1]." The various editors of Year Books, Horwood, Pike, Maitland, will have none of it, nor will anyone else that I know of. Maitland was at first inclined to believe that the Year Books were, the earliest of them, at any rate, something of the nature of students' note-books; note-books in which the students, learning their business in Court, jotted down what struck them individually as being of importance or of interest, as material for subsequent discussion amongst themselves. I do not know that he definitely formulated any other theory, but in the light of further know-ledge and fuller consideration he seemed disposed to revise this early opinion, for he subsequently wrote that the object of the report, the report of the Year Books, was, from the very first, "science, jurisprudence, the advancement of learning"; and these are not quite the terms in which one would generally speak of the jottings in a law-student's note-book. I quoted above some words of Sir Frederick Pollock's in which he refused to allow an official or even a semi-official character to the Year Books. In refusing even a semi-official character to them he was referring to a theory set out by Mr Pike. Any considered opinion which Mr Pike expresses on any question relating to the Year Books must be treated with great respect. Now, while Mr Pike was strong in his disbelief of the Year Books having any official character, he was somewhat inclined to believe that they might have had what might be called a semi-official origin. He was unwilling to believe that Plowden's statement, endorsed by Bacon and Coke and Blackstone, was without some sort of warrant, was nothing but a vain invention without any real historical foundation; and so he came to the conclusion that though the Year Books had no official authority they might have come from an official source. I think that this theory of Mr Pike's as to what was possible, I do not know that

[1] *Law Quarterly Review*, XXIX, p. 211.

I should be justified in calling it his actual belief, was based chiefly on the fact that we not infrequently find in our Year Books which are written mainly in French—in Anglo-Norman to be correct—extracts from the official Latin Plea Rolls, which extracts, one supposes, could not be made without the knowledge and consent of the clerk or officer who had the custody of these rolls. They were not open to general inspection. Faced by and fully recognizing the fact that all the manuscript Year Books which have descended to us have been found in circumstances which indicate that they were originally in private hands, and granting as beyond question that, whatever their authorship, they had no official recognition as part of the property of any Court, Mr Pike has argued very learnedly in support of this semi-official origin of the Year Books, but scarcely, I think, with complete conviction even to himself. I have not time here and now to review Mr Pike's arguments in support of this theory of the semi-official authorship of the Year Books, though they must certainly be read and considered by all who would qualify themselves for forming an opinion of their own upon a very difficult and knotty problem.

The question of the origin of the Year Books is really a double question; the question of the origin of the original Year Books, the original reports in the handwriting of the men who actually made the reports; and the question of the origin of the Year Books as we have them in manuscript now. No original Year Book, in the meaning which I have given to the term, exists, at any rate so far as anyone knows, nor did one ever exist within the time of anyone who has given thought to what the origin of such a book might be. Quite possibly, at the very first, they were, as Maitland was inclined to believe, something in the nature of students' note-books, or perhaps more likely of apprentices' note-books. The apprentices, I may remind those of you who are less familiar with the legal terminology of the Middle Age, were what to-day would be called barristers. They had not the right of audience in the Court of Common Bench, in which most of the cases reported in the Year Books were heard, but they had the right of audience in the other Courts, excluding the Common Pleas jurisdiction of the Commissions of General Eyre; and it was from them that the Serjeants were recruited. I think it likelier that these earliest reports were made by apprentices rather than students because they infer a knowledge of law and practice, a perception of an important point or ruling, much more likely to be characteristic of a barrister who had gone through the full course of professional study than of the student who had not yet acquired that fuller knowledge and ability to discriminate between what was really important and what was not. Let us grant then, without in the least asserting it, that the earliest notes were made by apprentices for their own private purposes. Now these notes were notes of what happened in the Common Bench, of the arguments, the objections, the rulings and judgments used and taken and made. These would never, one supposes, be of any use to an apprentice, so long as he remained an apprentice. But the note-taking apprentice looked forward to the day when he should become a Serjeant, when he should have the right to practise in the great Court of Common Bench. Then these notes which he had taken in his earlier days might become of the greatest use to him, showing him what had been the most successful and the least successful pleas in various circumstances, in what way a particular plea could best be met, a particular objection best refuted; what judgments might most hopefully be asked for in this case or in that; what rulings the Court had given on the various points of law that had been raised before them, what judgments, what instructive *obiter dicta* had come from the lips of the several Justices, and many another useful piece of knowledge besides. And I do not think that there is much difficulty in believing that these apprentices, being constantly in Court, were on sufficient terms of friendship with the clerks of the Court in charge of the rolls to be allowed now and again to look at the rolls and to make such short extracts from them as they wanted to make for the greater completeness of their notes. When the note-taking apprentice came to practise as a Serjeant he would find his old note-book most useful. It would be a sort of text-book of law and practice in which he could usually find something on the point which was exercising his mind. When he became a busy Serjeant he would no longer have the time or

opportunity for note-taking, and as his own notes were growing
older and perhaps a little out of date, he no doubt often wished
for more recent ones of the same kind. Then it probably occurred
to him that another generation of apprentices was still making
like notes with a like purpose in view. Could he get copies
of those notes? Could he arrange to get term by term copies
of the notes made by this apprentice or that? What this particular Serjeant of our imagination was thinking and what he
was wanting was what other Serjeants, probably all the Serjeants,
were thinking and wanting; and what a sufficient number of
people of sufficient influence want they usually find some means
of getting, especially if they are able and willing to pay for it.
Further, there are generally men with some command of capital
who get to hear of these wants and make it their business to
supply them if they think that they can do so profitably to themselves. Maybe the Serjeants themselves, maybe some men of
capital, it does not much matter to us which, recognizing the
demand for the continuation and multiplication of these Court
notes, of their possible expansion by the makers of them
rendering them more effective for their purpose, made provision for such expansion and for their circulation amongst
such Serjeants and others as wanted them and were willing
to pay for them. Suppose such a syndicate forming itself
on strictly commercial lines. What would it be likely to do?
They would look about them for two or three of the ablest
apprentices who were willing to be engaged and engage them to
attend the sittings of the Common Bench regularly, to jot down
on scraps of parchment just such facts, just such fragments of
dialogue and argument as will make it plain why the Serjeants
engaged in a case thought it worth while to venture upon this
or that plea; noting what pleas were in the end successful or
unsuccessful and why; noting in fact all those points of law and
practice a knowledge of which would form part of the necessary
equipment of counsel who wanted to deal as successfully as
possible with like cases in the future. These notes, made under
pressure and probably not fully intelligible to any but themselves, the apprentices would take home with them and decipher
and amplify and copy in a plain script. When these reporting

apprentices have made a fair copy of their amplified notes these copies will be collected by agents of the Syndicate or will be put into their hands somehow, and carried off to their *Scriptoria* or writing-rooms. In these *Scriptoria* will be gathered men who can write with reasonable rapidity and legibility, but whom the testimony of their work prevents us from crediting with much more than this. What happened then? Some one, we may suppose, will read the reporter's notes aloud. The scribes will follow with their pens the spoken words as accurately as they can, consistently with not taking overmuch trouble, and, one would imagine from what results they produced, never worrying themselves about getting a word which they had not caught overcertainly repeated; but they will not set down exactly what the reader read, unless, and it is not a very improbable supposition, he was as inclined to make slips as they were. A word will be misheard for another word that has a similar sound but a quite different meaning, and the wrong word will go down. That it happens to make nonsense is not the business of the scribes; at any rate they do not take it to be. Then people in those days did not write with the rapidity with which they do in these days of very liquid ink and perfectly flowing pens. And I may add parenthetically that if the mediaeval Year Books, with all their cryptic abbreviations and their various errors and corruptions had been written in a script at all comparable with a good deal of the writing one sees nowadays, they would be absolutely undecipherable by a modern student of them. Whatever their other faults and shortcomings may have been, the mediaeval professional scribes were, as a whole, excellent writers. What letters they chose to write they wrote completely, formed them completely, so that a man who has had some little experience of what they wrote can read it more easily and with greater certainty than he can read many a letter which comes to him to-day. I have suffered much at the hands of these mediaeval scribes, but I will give them their due. Owing to this slowness in writing some of the scribes were not able to make their pens keep pace with the reader's tongue, and they seem to have written sometimes from memories so flurried and confused by anxiety lest they should fall too hopelessly behind the reader that it is often but muddled copy which they turn out. A scribe, for instance, will suddenly recollect that he has omitted some sentence or half-sentence which the reader had read a moment or two before. He will then proceed to write it down, quite regardless of the fact that it is entirely out of place in the position in which he puts it; that it, in fact, makes nonsense of the immediate context. However, he has written it down somehow and somewhere and it is for his editor, six or seven hundred years afterwards, after much travail of soul to unravel the puzzle by recognizing what had happened, that the words which occur in some particular line ought to have been inserted two or three lines earlier. And so from inaccuracy of hearing, from careless-ness, from inability or neglect to follow the reader with the closeness necessary for accurate reproduction, we get a series of first variants from the same set of original notes. Each scribe has produced a version different from the original version and different from the versions of his fellows. What happened next, what became of this first series of variants? Judging from an order of mistakes to be found in a second series of variants quite different from such as are attributable to any of the causes which I have just suggested, mistakes that could not have occurred in copies made from dictation, I imagine that this is what happened. These first variants were distributed to scribes who copied them from inspection, not from dictation. They relied upon their eyes and not upon their ears, and I am afraid that they used the one set of organs as carelessly and uncritically as they used the other. They never thought of amending mistakes already made by the first set of scribes. They had enough to do in making fresh ones of their own. They would misread words in the text they were copying. They would come to some cryptic abbreviation which they could not understand and instead of copying it exactly as it stood they turned it into something which nobody could either read or understand. They would copy their text down to some particular word and then raising their eyes again to their book would catch sight of the same word occurring lower down than the place where they had left off and would then mechani-cally continue copying from that second occurrence, leaving out all that intervened, be it much or little.

If we happen to possess another manuscript from which the writer has not allowed these particular words or lines to fall out, we suffer no great harm; but we do not always possess such a supplementary text. Now and again these omissions occur in circumstances which make them more serious and bewildering than they would be if they were nothing more than omissions. You will remember that our Year Books are written in dialogue form. Counsel on one side lays down some proposition, advances some argument, or, maybe, makes some statement of fact. Counsel on the other side then does what he can to make naught of his opponent's speech. Now if the omitted text should happen to include, as it not infrequently does, the latter part of a speech by counsel on one side and the earlier part of the speech in reply by counsel on the other side, you may imagine the result. We get a speech in which the speaker seems to be advancing arguments merely as a preliminary to showing how rotten they are; to be stating facts for no other purpose than immediately contradicting what he has just said. Lapses of this kind are apt to be distracting, until one has grasped what has really happened. In this way we get a second series of variants, all of which, together with the first set, are lineally descended from a single original report. And so the process went on, the individual members of each series varying amongst themselves, and, as a class, varying increasingly from the original report. And there may have been two, or even more, original reports, reporting different arguments, different rulings by the Court, different details of various kinds, according to each reporter's point of view as to the relative importance of this or that aspect of the case. And from each of these original reports we shall get a similar lineal series of variants. The copies so made were, I suppose, at once put upon the market, just as they were first written, mistakes, repetitions, omissions, and all. But we are a long way yet from accounting for the Year Books as we have them. They are, as you know, not detached reports of terms, but shorter or longer collections of the reports may be of many successive years, may be only of a few years here and a few years there, with gaps of longer or shorter extent, with, perhaps, reports of one or two quite detached terms. How did these collections as we have them to-day get themselves put together? What was the genesis of our surviving manuscript Year Books? They are a long way off the terminal reports which we have supposed the professional scribes of the commercial *Scriptoria* to be constantly turning out[1].

These Year Books of ours, those earlier ones, at any rate, which have as yet been the most carefully considered and studied, were all written a good many years after the date of the cases which they report. Some of them, containing reports over a long series of years, ten or a dozen, were, one may say it certainly, I think, individually written by the same scribe within a restricted time, for the character of the handwriting remains the same throughout. The scribes of the surviving Year Books one seems justified in saying surely were not the original scribes of the *Scriptoria*. The terminal reports of these scribes of the *Scriptoria* grew scarcer as the years went by, becoming gradually destroyed by the wear and tear of daily use and reference. It occurred to one or two or several scribes of later years that it would be a useful work, and not without profit to themselves, to collect those detached terminal reports so far as they could and make fresh copies of them as a united and consecutive whole. Such compilations of them would be more convenient for study and reference than a bundle of detached reports of terms, ever accumulating and growing ever more inconvenient, through their number, for purposes of reference, even for carrying about when counsel wanted them for use in Court. Or it might be that here again some sort of commercial syndicate came into action, and employed professional scribes to make these compilations and transcripts. But whether the work were done by individual copyists acting on their own initiative or by scribes working for pay by the direction of others, or by men of both classes, does not much matter. But that something of the kind

---

[1] Mr G. J. Turner has carefully considered the question of the origin of the Year Books as they survive in manuscript form and has evolved the nucleus of a theory to which he has given the name of the "pamphlet" theory; but he guards himself by saying that this theory cannot as yet (1911) be stated in very precise language. What he says on the matter will be found in the Introduction to vol. VI of the Selden Society's *Year Book Series*. I do not know that he has since then carried the matter any further.

happened, was bound to happen if the reports had shown themselves to be of any use or profit at all, we may safely assert. And when these compilations and transcripts had been put together and fairly copied as often as copies might be called for, the need for the original separate reports of terms would disappear, and it would not be worth while preserving any longer those separate reports, and they would naturally disappear, as they have done this long while past. That is pretty much the story of the manuscript Year Books from first to last as I read it. They had, I am inclined to think, a commercial origin. They were continued; the sectional reports, if one may so describe them, were collected and copied and put into circulation as volumes of varying bulk because experience showed that it was a good business proposition. I do not believe that there was ever anything either official or semi-official about them, but that they were produced by one set of people or another for purely commercial reasons. I would not, of course, go so far as to assert that no student ever made a transcript of one of these volumes for his own private use, adding, perhaps, an annotation or a query here and there, and that some of the collections we possess to-day are such privately made transcripts, or even privately made copies of such transcripts.

As to the possibility or probability of students making transcripts for their own private use only, I may say parenthetically that I have not found any evidence to show that there were facilities in England for borrowing and copying manuscripts equal to those to be found in some of the continental Universities, where a system of what we call to-day circulating libraries existed. Prices were high and manuscripts were not very plentiful, and it was felt that the poor student was sorely let and hindered in his studies in consequence. In the fourteenth century, and before and after, no bookseller could carry on business within the jurisdiction of the University of Paris without the University's licence, and the University made its own conditions on granting such licences. In 1323 the University published a regulation compelling all booksellers to lend out their manuscripts on hire, and they were further enjoined to compile catalogues of these and to hang them up in their shops with a notice of the respective prices charged for the loan of them. The University itself assessed the prices which might be charged according to the length of the manuscript, but in no case was more than a few pence charged; though, of course, a few pence in 1323 meant a good deal more than a few pence to-day, so that the borrower might know beforehand what he would be called upon to pay. The student borrowing a manuscript was allowed to transcribe it, and nothing appears in the regulations as to the length of time he was allowed to keep it in his possession[1]. I have seen some of these lists of manuscripts and schedules of prices as they were set up in the booksellers' shops in Paris in the fourteenth century—the originals are still in existence—and one does not gather from them that there was any very flourishing law school in Paris in those days. The books named in the lists, and I suppose that these would be the books most in demand, are nearly all theological works of one kind and another. There is a little metaphysical philosophy, but no law. Similar regulations were in force in, certainly, the Universities of Bologna, Toulouse and Vienna. One reason I have for doubting whether any such system existed in mediaeval England, or that, if it did, it embraced manuscripts of our Year Books, is the fact that if any of the manuscripts borrowed under it were found to be faulty or imperfect they were, on the student's report, denounced by the University and a fine was imposed upon the bookseller who had lent them. Any licensing authority in mediaeval England having to deal in such fashion with the manuscript Year Books would have had no idle time nor have lacked opportunities in plenty of growing moderately rich on the fines which the misfeasances of the copyists gave ample and righteous cause for imposing.

But before I leave my present subject I must say something about the head-notes, or rather side-notes, marginal notes, which occur in our manuscripts. These vary, when there is any side-note at all, and there is not always one, from the merest catchword such as *Garde* or *Douere* to an attempt to set out in as few words as possible the essential facts of the case and the

[1] On these matters Chevillier's *Origines de l'Imprimerie de Paris* (4to, 1694), pp. 301 and onwards, may be consulted.

point of law which was settled. We have, as I have said, groups of manuscripts which so closely resemble each other that it seems certain that they come from the same parent source, from the same original. In these closely related reports, though the text is practically identical in them, yet the side-notes vary widely. The text in them all comes from the same original reporter; the side-notes have come from other sources; each note from some subsequent annotator who has considered his text with more intelligence than the mere copyists did. These notes provide us with much matter for speculation. They are, in all seeming, in the same handwriting as the text of the reports which they annotate; and, one would say, were written at the same time. What I want to indicate is this; it is only theory, of course, but the facts seem to point strongly to it. The manuscripts which we possess, the manuscripts with which we have to work, are copies of manuscripts which in the first instance were the work of the professional scribe. These copies passed into the possession of the practising lawyer or intelligent student who studied them, and then did his best to set out in the fewest possible words what each case seemed to determine. Then this particular set of reports with its annotations was copied by some one; and that is the manuscript which we have to-day. Copies of the same set of reports, made by the professional scribes, went into the hands of different lawyers or students, and each individual possessor made his own notes. It occurred to one of such to make a quite different note from that which it occurred to another to make. It would have been strange, indeed, if two independent annotators had expressed themselves in identical or nearly identical words. Let me now, before I go any further, give a few examples of these widely variant notes to reports so closely resembling each other as to make it fairly certain that they were all copies, in longer or shorter descent, from the same original report. The black-letter editions, I may remark incidentally, uniformly omit these side-notes, printing nothing beyond the merest catchword, where they print anything at all. In an action of annuity brought by Robert Well against Thomas Cayley[1] (7 Edward II) the note in the manuscript from which

[1] *Year Book Series* (Selden Society), XVI, p. 50.

the black-letter edition is printed is thus: "Annuyte ou le defendant dit qe le pleyntif fut homme marie par qei etc. Et il ne counta mie par seisine pur ceo qe le fet ne voleit pas dedi." In other closely related reports of the same case we get these variant notes: "De annuite en quele le defendant se aueyt oblige al pleyntif si la qil ly auoit puruewe de benefice qil voleit receyuere ou le defendant dit qe le pleyntif auoit pris femme par qei etc."; and "Annuete graunte par celes paroles quousque per me vel per heredes meos promotus fuerit ad competens beneficium quod duxerit acceptandum ou le demandant prist femme." I am not sure that the gist of the case would be apparent to a modern student from any of these notes, a consideration which may excuse the printers of the black-letter editions for their practice of uniformly omitting them. And, no doubt, the original annotators in their efforts to be brief did often succeed only, so far, at any rate, as any one else was concerned, in becoming obscure. But they knew what they wanted themselves and did not consider posterity. I attach some importance to these variant notes to closely connected manuscripts and the bearing which they may have, when they have been more fully studied, on the dark question of the origin of the manuscript Year Books as we have them; and I will give a few more examples. One Richard Olive brought a writ of admeasurement of pasture against the Prior of Bridlington[1]. The note in the manuscript from which the black-letter edition is printed is: "Amesurement de pasture porte vers vn Priour ou il fut persone de la ville ou etc. et pur ceo qe il ne fut pas nome persone le bref sabaty." The fuller note in a very closely related manuscript is: "De admensuracione pasture porte vers vn persone qe tynt partie des tenemenz mis en vewe cum de dreit de sa eglise et partie cum lay fee et ne fut pas nome persone en le bref par quei le bref se abati." In an action about tithes between an Abbot and a Prior[2] the note in one manuscript is: "Annuyte entre .ij. persones de seinte eglise ou dymes furent tournez en vn Annuete issint lay fee et Labbe charge lui et ses successours en cel annuete." In two other manuscripts, both closely related with this one, the notes are respectively: "Dannuyte ou variaunce fut chalange entre conte et lespecialte et la iurisdiccioun chalenge pur ceo qil fut issaunt des dimes garbes," and "Annuite qe vn abbe demanda de vn priour par resoun de dymes qe furent en debat entre eux ou la especialte qe le abbe bota auaunt ne lya poynt les successours le priour." One could quote similarly variant notes to closely related manuscripts by the score, but no present purpose could be served by doing so. The emergent thought is that those surviving manuscripts which have no side-note at all or merely a catchword like *Garde* or *Intrusion* stand earlier in the pedigree than those more elaborately annotated; but to confirm or to confute any such theory would call for a much closer and more prolonged study of the actual words and verbal variations of the related texts than I have been able to give to them. But I am inclined to believe that these side-notes may have something to reveal to us which we do not yet know.

That is something like the story of how our manuscript Year Books came to exist in the form in which we have them to-day, as I read it. They appear to have descended from daily notes made hurriedly in circumstances not very favourable to accurate reporting by the apprentices of the law. These notes, possibly after having been revised and amplified while the memory of each day's happenings was still fresh in the reporter's mind, were copied from dictation in some commercial *Scriptorium*, and from this first set of copies made from dictation other copies were made from them by scribes who wrote down what they saw or thought they saw, and not what they heard as did the first set. These reports were probably put on sale term by term. Collections of them, of varying size, with missing parts here and there, were made by one person or another, and these individual collections, made up of reports in the handwriting of any number of scribes, according to their size, were transcribed as a consecutive whole by, as a rule, a single scribe; and so transcribed, it seems not unreasonable to suppose, from commercial motives. But I am not here doing more than offering to you what seem fairly plausible suggestions as to the origin of these Books. So far from asserting anything at all in this connexion, I speak doubtfully and uncertainly, because the whole matter remains at present so full of doubts, so full of uncertainties. Critical study of the Year Books is as yet but a young study. It has concentrated itself so far as it has yet gone on the earlier books alone. When the manuscripts, both the earlier and the later ones, have been more closely and thoroughly studied and examined, with the problem of the story of their origin and development in the student's mind, with a sharp eye for any chance marginal note or scribe's casual annotation, it is not very unlikely that some fact or statement throwing some light on that problem may be noted; and the more we know the more likely we are to be able to infer with some confidence what we do not know from what, through much travail, we have come to know. And so I hope that some day the story of the origin and development of those unique treasures of ours, the old Year Books, may be told by someone, in the light of fuller knowledge, with much more confidence and certainty than I have felt able even to suggest it to you to-day.

III

THE PRINTED EDITIONS OF THE YEAR BOOKS

WHEN I began to turn my thoughts to the preparation of this lecture on the printed editions of the Year Books a certain remark of Maitland's obtruded itself, rather disturbingly, into my mind. "To say much of the old editions of the Year Books," he once wrote, "seems unnecessary. Those who have attempted to read them know how bad, how incorrigibly bad, they are... of mere, sheer nonsense those old black-letter books are but too full[1]." At another time he spoke of them as "that hopeless mass of corruption[2]." This seems to leave me faced by the unpleasant dilemma of either detaining you here to waste your time listening to the babbling of a meandering stream of unnecessary talk about mere, sheer nonsense, or of asking you straightway to disperse yourselves to less unprofitable occupations. And I cannot bring myself to believe that either of these alternatives ever came within the contemplation of the Founder of the Sandars Readership. Yet one remembers for one's encouragement that the unnecessary is not always or necessarily the uninteresting, nor wholly unprofitable. And there certainly should be something of interest to be found in the story of the printing in the Gothic character of that long series of Year Books which were the study of generations of our older English lawyers, which were, indeed, the only form in which these old books were accessible to them with their wealth of instruction on the gradual forging of our common law into shape, of all the difficulties which had to be overcome before this or that principle which is now generally admitted and recognized was firmly established. So I hope that I may find something that may be worth saying, something not altogether without interest, about the story of the old black-letter printed editions of the Year Books. In some way we may look upon them as a by-product of the tail end of

---

[1] Selden Society's *Year Book Series*, I, p. xxi.
[2] *Collected Papers*, I, p. 484.

the great Renaissance of the fifteenth century, helped to birth
by the introduction of the art of printing into England. And
while we are talking and thinking of them we shall, at any rate,
get some glimpses of the men who made them, of our earliest
English printers, of the work they thought it worth their while
to do and where they did it. We shall see in some sort of shadow-
land those houses in mediaeval Fleet Street and by the Thames-
side, the names and approximate positions of which are set out
on title-page or in colophon, wherein these old volumes were
printed, we shall learn something of the way in which the several
volumes were put together; and perhaps we may pick up odd
scraps of not uninteresting information about other matters as
well.

The first printer in England, as everyone knows, was William
Caxton, and he was not only the first printer in England but
he was also the first English printer. He had to go abroad, of
course, to learn his business, but he was an Englishman, born
in Kent, while his immediate successors as printers in England
were foreigners. I wish I could persuade myself that Caxton,
the first printer Englishman, had printed any of our English
Year Books, but I cannot. For at least two reasons I could wish
that he had. One could wish that these peculiar treasures of
England had first been set in type by an Englishman; and then
there is some sort of a magic glamour about everything that
Caxton printed. The fact that a book was printed by him is
sufficient in itself to create an interest in that book, to set biblio-
graphers and people interested in our literature talking and
writing about it. I sometimes think that if Caxton had printed
a volume or two of our old Year Books the Year Books as a whole
might now have been much better remembered and known than
they have been these two centuries past. Some of Caxton's
books have been reprinted in facsimile. If he had printed a Year
Book we might have had that re-printed in facsimile, and it
might have revived an interest in the Year Books in far wider
circles than those to which modern Year Book study has so far
succeeded in reaching. But Caxton does not seem to have been
attracted by law. He printed works dealing with religion and
morality and philosophy; he printed poetry, romances, history
of a sort, translations from the classics and all manner of other

things. We know of some sixty-four or sixty-five books that issued from his press, but with the possible exception of a few fragments of statutes of Richard III and Henry VII there is nothing amongst them that deals with law.

The first real law printer in England was William Machlinia, but he was not an Englishman. He is supposed to have come from Mechlin and to have taken his name from that city. He had his press somewhere in Holborn, near Fleet Bridge—*iuxta pontem qui vulgariter dicitur Flete brigge*. He began printing Year Books some seven or eight years after the introduction of printing into England, and he led off Year Book printing not from the earliest manuscripts in existence, but from the latest, almost contemporary ones. Machlinia put no dates of publication on his books, but it was probably in 1482 or 1483 that he printed books of 33, 34, 35, 36 and 37 Henry VI, only some thirty years after the hearing of the actions reported in them. Why he should have selected these late years for publication in preference to earlier ones cannot now be determined. Manuscripts of them were probably commoner than those of further back years, intruded themselves more upon his notice, and would be likely to be in better condition. Any way, the first Year Books printed were those which had been written originally only some fifty years before the Year Books came to an end. It is probable that besides the years I have named Machlinia printed also the twentieth year of Henry VI. Ames and Herbert and Dibdin do not credit it to him, but the catalogue of the Library of Exeter College, Oxford, does, on the strength of its being bound up with the undoubted Machlinia of the thirty-fourth year—the only one of these books printed by Machlinia which bears his name, and the similarity of the type of the two years. Other law books which Machlinia printed were perhaps two editions of Littleton's *Tenures* and some collections of statutes. He seems to have printed all that he did print without having received any licence; at any rate none has ever been found. It may be that it took the King or his advisers some time before they discovered the expediency of restricting printing to licensed printers. The next on the roll of printers in England was Wynkyn de Worde, who came from Lorraine to work in Caxton's house, after whose death he set up in business for himself. He printed several law books, amongst which was Fitzherbert's *Grand Abridgement*, which though not technically a Year Book is made up of extracts from many Year Books. This was in 1516. He also printed in 1496 an edition of Lyndwood's *Provinciales*, and some other law books. His earliest books he printed at Westminster, probably in the same chapel in which Caxton had his press. His later ones were printed at the "Sign of the Sun" in Fleet Street. He turned out a great deal of work of all kinds of literature, publishing in his time 408 volumes. He died probably in 1534. Richard Pynson, who printed from 1493 to 1528, was the first systematic printer of Year Books. His earliest dated edition is 3 Henry VI, dated 12th October, 1510, but four of his undated pieces have been assigned by competent authority to the last ten years of the fifteenth century. Only seven of his Year Books are dated, and some fifty or perhaps fifty-five editions bear his name. He worked for some time in some sort of conjunction with Robert Redman. The nature of the relationship between them is not very plain; whether there was anything in the nature of a partnership, or whether Redman merely carried on his own independent work in Pynson's house. On 10th March, 1534, Redman published the first year of the Quadragesms[1], which he says in a prefatory address: "To the studentes of the Lawe" had not been truely printed by Richard Pynson or any other printer. "I therfore by the help of my frende[2] haue caused this boke (thus as ye see) to shewe hym selfe to the lyght[3]." He

---

[1] *I.e.* the years 40–50 Edward III.
[2] Ames suggests that the reference here is to Pynson.
[3] It seems worth while appending here the whole text of this address. It is unsigned, and is printed on the back of the title-page.
"To the studentes of the Lawe.

   Often tymes ponderynge with my selfe what commodyte it is to the studentes of the lawe, aswel as to the studentes of other sciences, to haue theyr bokes truly prentyd and well set out, and howe it amaseth them whan they study any boke of the law which is nat truely wryten or prentyd, for be the mater (wherof it entreateth) neuer so frutful, yet it is therby greatly defaced and emblemished. In auoydyng of which mischiefe, dyuers haue done theyr payne and labour about the pryntyng of sondry yeres, wherof (I thynke I may say) some haue ben fyrnyshed so that nothyng lacketh which industry myght have holpen,...And forasmoche as this yere called Quadragesimus of Edward the Thyrde is greatly bosted and noted of some studentes, to be a very principall good yere: and some other (as they say) though they often-tymes haue attempted, haue nat throughly studyed, or at leest nat so profyted

also printed the second year of the Quadragesms, 41 Edward III. Now Pynson himself had printed these two particular years, and whether he was a little nettled by Redman's observation that the two years which he printed had not been truely printed by Richard Pynson or any other printer, or whether he considered that Redman was encroaching too much on his own branch of work, one cannot tell; or was annoyed with him for using his own device[1]; but for some reason or other the two associates presently quarrelled. Redman had published an edition of Littleton's *Tenures*, and when some time afterwards Pynson printed one too he had some unpleasant things to say about Redman. His own edition, he says, is more correct and ornate than that which issued from the hands of Robert Redman, "sed uerius Rudeman, quia inter mille homines rudiorem haud facile inuenies"; and he goes on, with considerable bitterness of diction, to accuse him of incompetency and ignorance[2]; and in

in the same, peraduenture bycause it was nat by Rychard Pynson or any other prenter, before this tyme truely prented,...I therfore by the help of my frende haue caused this boke (thus as ye see) to shewe hym selfe in the lyght. Which if ye ernestly do rede and study I thynke the paynetakers in this doying worthy some prayse or commendation. And if ye so do accepte and take it with good herte, ye shall encourage nat onely the setterforth herof to do some further enterpryse, but also parauenture some other better lerned to take on hand the lyke or better deuyse, to your great profyte and commodyte. Valete."

[1] The suggestion that Redman's appropriation of one of Pynson's principal devices with his well-known monogram and his affixing of it without apology to a number of books printed by himself was a possible cause of Pynson's irritation was made by Ames. Herbert, however, in revising Ames's work, disagrees, on the ground that he cannot find any instance of Redman using the device until a somewhat later period. Dibdin, in revising Ames and Herbert, continues Ames's suggestion and omits Herbert's comment. And there I must leave the matter.

[2] The date of this edition by Pynson of the *Tenures* is 1525. On the last leaf is the following address by Pynson to the reader. "Richardus Pynsonus regius Impressor lectori salutem. En tibi Candide lector iam castigatior (ni fallor) Littiltonus occurrit. Curaui ut e calcographia mea non solum emendatior, uerum etiam elegantioribus typis ornatior prodeat in lucem: quam elapsus est e manibus Rob. Redman, sed uerius Rudeman, quia inter mille homines rudiorem haud facile inuenies. Miror profecto unde nunc tandem se fateatur typographum, nisi forte quum diabolus sutorem nauclerum, et illum calcographum fecit. Olim nebulo ille profitebatur se bibliopolam tam peritum quam unquam ab Vtopia exiluit: Bene scit liber est qui prae se speciem libri fert, praeterea fere nihil: tamen ausus est scurra polliceri, sua cura reuerendas ac sanctas leges Angliae scite uereque omnes imprimere. Vtrum uerba dare usus, an uerax sit, tu Littiltono legendo s. sua cura ac diligentia excuso, illico uidear. Vale."

an edition of Magna Charta of 1527 the like strain of abuse is maintained. Redman, however, appears to have taken it all in good part, returning no other answers to Pynson's abuse than "Si Deus nobiscum quis contra nos?" It is pleasant to know that there is good reason to believe that Pynson and Redman were fully reconciled before Pynson died.

We now come to Richard Tottell, who has several claims to distinction. In the first place he seems to have been of all men of whom I know anything the most uncertain how his own name should be written or spelled. He has given us four variants of his Christian name, Richard. Nothing but the most perverse ingenuity could very well have devised more. Sometimes he prints it "Richard," according to the modern custom: sometimes "Rychard," and sometimes he adds an "e" to these forms. He has given us nine variants of his surname: Tathyll, Tothill, Tottle, Tottele, Tottell, Tottil, Tottill, Tottyl, Tottyll. And so we seem to have his own authority for writing his full name in thirty-two different ways. And I doubt if you can say as much of any other man. Then Tottell was the first, and so far as I know the only man, who ever was granted an exclusive right to print what law books he chose to print. Everyone else was forbidden to print those which Tottell had taken to himself. You will find his patent set out in Dugdale's *Origines Juridiciales*[1] in these terms:

A special license to Richard Tathille, Citizen. Stationer and Printer of London, for him and his assigns, to imprint for the space of seven years next ensuing the date hereof all manner of Books of the Temporal Law called the Common Law, so as the copies be allowed and adjudged meet to be printed by one of the Justices of the Law or two Serjeants or three apprentices of the law, whereof the one to be a Reader in Court. And that none other shall imprint any book which the said Richard Tathille shall first take and imprint during the said term upon pain of forfeiture of all such books.

This patent is dated 12th April, 7 Edward VI. I hope that you have noted the interesting little equation contained in the licence, that the opinion of one Justice as to the merits of a law book is worth as much as that of two Serjeants or of three ordinary barristers, even when one of these three has, from his

[1] P. 59 (ed. of 1666).

knowledge of law, been appointed a Reader or Teacher in an Inn of Court. Tottell received a second licence[1], dated 1st May, 3 Philip and Mary, by which he was authorized "to imprint or cause to be imprinted, for the space of seaven years next ensuing, all manner of Books which touch or concern the Common Law, whether allready imprinted or not." But from the particular point of view from which we are looking at him just now perhaps Tottell's greatest claim to distinction was that he was the printer of Year Books *par excellence*. It seems but a sorry tribute to the great work he did to have to say in a lecture upon our early Year Book printers that it was too great a one to set out the particular details of it. But that is the real truth, as you will understand when I tell you that there are about 225 known editions of separate years or groups of years which bear his imprint or can be certainly attributed to his press. To give just fifteen seconds to a bare mention of each of these editions would take up almost the whole of the time limited for the whole lecture. I can only summarize his great work. Between 1553 and 1591 he not only reprinted all the years already published, but he also printed for the first time all the other years which have been included in subsequent editions, that is in subsequent editions of reports of the reigns of which any reports at all had been published. He published no reports of Edward II or of Richard II. He printed so freely and so lessened the price at which he was able to put the Year Books on the market that he had evidently made them a popular and commercially profitable section of his output. Besides so greatly excelling all previous printers in the number of Year Books he printed, Tottell originated, it is scarcely too much to say, the system of printing and publishing the Year Books in more or less extensive groups of years. Before his time the years had always been printed separately, or, at the most, two years together. The one exception was the first eight years of Henry VII, which were printed together without any date or printer's name, probably by Pynson about 1505. Tottell had not been long at work before, in 1553, he printed the years 1–14 Henry IV as one book. In 1555 he printed together 1–21 Henry VI; in 1556 he printed

---

[1] *Origines Juridiciales*, p. 60.

the ten years of Edward III known as the Quadragesms; in 1561 and again in 1580 he printed editions of the *Liber Assisarum*; in 1562, the first ten years of Edward III, and in 1563 all the years of Henry V. Each of these several groups of years was published as a whole, as the same as a single volume. Perhaps this system of printing several years in one volume made the price of that volume larger than a sufficient number of people were willing to pay; perhaps there were other practical objections to it. I cannot say. But, with the exceptions of the groups of years which I have just mentioned, Tottell did all the rest of his great output of Year Books after the earlier fashion, one year at a time. I may note here that the period of printing individual years may be said to have lasted from 1481 to 1591, something more than a century. There was, indeed, one single year printed separately after that time, but one only; the report that has acquired the name of the Long Quinto, the quite exceptionally long report of 5 Edward IV. But the Long Quinto is such a long report as to make no inconsiderable volume in itself. With one exception by Robert Redman, to which I will refer presently, none of these early printers prefixed anything of the nature of a preface or introduction to the Reports they published. They made no reflexions upon the value of their work, no sort of commendation of it, no hint as to the provenance of their original manuscripts. Tottell does indeed say in a note on the title-page of his edition of the Quadragesms of 1565: "Anni omnes a mendis quibus miserrime scatebant repurgati et suo nitori Restituti." In an edition of Magna Charta printed by him in 1556 he gives us his views on the earlier editions of the Year Books and upon his own, which I think that I may very properly reproduce:

How unperfit the bokes of the lawes of England were before, what price the scarcenes had raysed, the most part mervelously mangled & no smale part no wher to be gotten there be enow, though I rehease it not, that do freshlye remember & can truely witness. Likewise how, sithens I toke in hand to serve your uses, that imperfections have been supplied, the price so eased as the scarcenes no more hindreth but that ye have them as chepe (notwithstandinge the common dearth of these times) as when they were most plentiful, the print much pleasanter to the eye in the bokes of yeres than any that ye have ben yet served with, paper & margine as good & as faire as the best, but much better & fairer then the most, no smal nomber by me set forth newly in print that before were scant to be found in writing. I nede not my self to report it.

For the exact truth thereof, my copies I might wel follow as thei were, but I could not my self correct them as they ought to be. Therefore in some workes, where I could, with my entreatie or cost, procure learneden helpe, ye have them not smally amended; in some other where I could not, yet dare I answer they are nothing appeired.

I have certainly had neither the inclination nor the time myself to put to the proof Tottell's claims that his editions were printed with a correctness excelling that of the editions by other printers. All I can say of my own knowledge is that when I have found some obvious corruption in one edition and have referred to another in the hope that I might find something more intelligible, I have been invariably disappointed. May be I have been unfortunate. But I take it that there was very little emendation done; and as there is no indication from what original manuscript authority these printed editions are made, it is practically impossible to make any attempt to correct the printed text by the manuscript.

At the end of his edition of 1534 of the first year of the Quadragesms, 40 Edward III, Redman printed this note:

Telos. Forasmoch as most men do not prayse any matter whiche is any thyng obscure & not playne to declare y[e] entent of hym which is the maker: therfore gentyl and louyng reder ye shal understande that in al the cases of this forsaid yere, where as ye find ony crosse, there immediately after the same crosse doth begynne myne addicion or fantasye, and contynueth no forther than to the next Parafe. After the which parafe the resydue of the case doth procede, none other wyse than it was by the reporters fyrst reported, yf the case be not then at an ende. Secondly ye shall note the Justices names, to whose wordes ye must chiefly gyve credens before the saynges of ony of the Sargeantes.

Then follow the names of the Justices and those of eight Serjeants. Then there is a short table of "the notable faultes escaped in the printyng." These "addicions or fantasyes" of which Redman in this note speaks are nothing more than references to later cases of a like nature with those to the reports of which they are appended. Tottell, in his edition of 1565, reproduces this note verbatim. He makes, so to speak, the "addicions and fantasyes" his own, and seems to claim all credit for them for himself. The point of this is that it is some sort of a proof of the mechanical way in which these sixteenth century printers produced their editions of the Year Books. They appear merely to have got hold of some earlier edition and re-printed it exactly as it stood, errors and all, and, as in this par-ticular case, with matter which the later printer was not entitled to print as his own, at any rate without some explanation. And the reproduction *verbatim* by Tottell of this note of Redman's seems a fair proof of the mechanical and unintelligent way in which the printing and publishing of Year Books was done in those days.

The earlier printers of Year Books gave little or no attention to making their foliation correspond with that of earlier editions. For instance, Pynson's undated edition of 3 Henry VI has fifty-eight folios, his edition of 1510 has fifty-two; Smyth's edition has fifty-eight and Tottell's reprints all have fifty-six. Machlinia's 34 Henry VI has ninety-one folios, Pynson's has fifty-eight and Tottell's has fifty-four. The unnamed (though probably Machlinia's) 35 Henry VI has fifty-six folios, the probable Pynson has seventy; Redman's edition has seventy and Tottell's sixty-four. From Tottell's time onward each folio of a reprint generally contained almost exactly the same matter as the corresponding folio of the edition re-printed. But errors in pagination are frequent, and it is fortunate that in citations of cases the regnal year, term and number of the plea are fre-quently given.

John Rastell, who was working his press from 1517 to 1533, was the first to print the *Liber Assisarum*. His edition bears no date. Rastell often wrote poems to books published by him, and he furnished his edition of the *Liber Assisarum* with a long prologue.

Prologus Iohīs rastel in laudem legū Quod Respublica non usque adeo resplendescat pompa diuitiarum aut viribus aut honoris fastigio: sed ex bonis Legibus summum perfectionis gradum sola conse-quatur.

He works out this thesis in English, and concludes that

they that exercise and busi thēself ī makīgg laws in ordring or writīg of lawes in lerning of lawes or teching lawes or by iust and trewe executing of lawes be thos parsons that gretly incres & multiply the comēwell.

Then he goes on to say something of great bibliographical interest in connexion with the *editio princeps* of Fitzherbert's *Grand Abridgement*.

We propose further to put in print a nother boke which by goddis grace shall be bett' done & with mich more dylygēce thā this present boke of assises that is now done & fynisshyd in grete hast, which other boke shall be a grete boke of abbregementz of arguyd casis rulyd in many yeres of diuers sondry kyngys cōteyning vi or vii C. leuis of grete paper with diuers grete tables lōging thereto cōtriued orderid & nōberid with figures of algorism for the grete expedeciō & fortheraūce of the studes of this law.

From this we may reasonably infer two things. First, that the date of this edition of the *Liber Assisarum* very shortly preceded the first publication of Fitzherbert's *Abridgement*, the first volume of which was probably published in 1514. No printer's name appears anywhere in this edition. Dibdin is inclined to attribute it to Wynkyn de Worde; but considering Rastell's statement in his prologue to the *Liber Assisarum* and the fact that both books are printed from like type, it seems more than probable that Rastell had something to do with the printing of the first edition of the *Abridgement*. John Rastell had a son, William, of whom it will not be irrelevant to say something here. He was a student at Oxford, but left the University without taking a degree. He was admitted a student of Lincoln's Inn on 12th September, 1532, and was called to the Bar there in the Trinity Term of 1539. He was made a Bencher in 1546, a Reader in 1547, and he was Treasurer of the Inn in 1549 and 1554. In 1550, it may be incidentally noted, he was fined £10 for going into foreign parts without permission of the Governors[1]. In October, 1555, he was created a Serjeant, and just three years later he was appointed a Justice of the Queen's Bench, not a month before Queen Mary died. Between leaving Oxford and being called to the Bar at

[1] *Black Books of Lincoln's Inn*, I, p. 293.

Lincoln's Inn he appears to have been engaged in the printing business. Amongst other books he published two editions of the Register of Writs in 1531, and in 1534 a volume containing the *Natura Brevium*, the old tenures, Littleton's *Tenures* and other legal tracts. But what gives him in this present connexion his special interest is the fact that he is credited with being the author of the well-known and frequently reprinted *Termes de la Ley*[1]. He printed no Year Books. Robert Redman (who was printing from 1525 to 1540) published nearly fifty different years of Edward III, Henry VI, Edward IV, Richard III and Henry VII, mostly separately, though he issued the first seven years of Henry VII as a single publication. His contemporary, Thomas Berthelet, printed 21–28 Edward III as an entire publication, as the signatures and pages are in regular succession; and the years 7, 8, 14 and 15 of Henry VII as separate issues. Robert Wyer printed only one year, 9 Henry IV. William Myddleton (1541–1548) printed ten years of Henry VI, four of Edward IV, three of Henry VII, and the twenty-seventh year of Henry VIII. Henry Smyth (about 1545, but none of his Year Books are dated) printed eight years of Henry VI. William Powell (1547–1567) printed the books of 9 Henry V; 11, 12, 13 and 17 Edward IV; an edition of the Long Quinto in 1532, and 12 and 13 Henry VII in 1548. In 1596 Jane Yetsweirt reprinted 1–10 Edward III in one volume.

In 1606 the Company of Stationers printed an edition of the *Liber Assisarum*; in 1609 the first half of Henry VI. They did nothing more for ten years, and then in 1619 they printed the second half of Edward III, and in that same year and the following one they reprinted the years of Edward V, Richard III, Henry VII and Henry VIII. For the next fifty years no Year Book was printed by anyone. Perhaps the supply had overtaken the demand. By 1678 the demand seems to have overtaken the supply, and there is a note in Clarke's *Bibliotheca Legum* that a fairly complete set in ten volumes sold about that time for £40, then a very considerable sum of money. In 1678 George Sawbridge, William Rawlins and Saul Roycroft, assigns of

---

[1] *Athenae Oxonienses* (ed. P. Bliss, 1813), I, 344 and Ames's *Typographical Antiquities* (1790), I, p. 474.

Richard and Edward Atkyns, printed for T. Bassett, J. Wright and James Collins—it is right that the names of all these men should be recorded—the Year Books of the whole of Edward II, as well as extracts from the Exchequer Memoranda of Edward I. None of the years of Edward II had as yet been printed by anyone. To this volume was prefixed a Preface in these terms:

Reader, Thou hast here made public for the common use and benefit the Old Book of the Years and Terms of Edward the Second; a volume much and long desired by the most learned of the Gown, who could best discern the Advantage that would be reaped from so Authentique a Work, and sufficiently recommended to the world by the Judgment that hath been made of it by such as have known the use and value of it in the copy...there is some small variety in the copies. Farewell.

No signature is added. The Imprimatur, signed by Chief Justice Finchden and eleven other Justices and Serjeants, runs:

For the encouragement of so chargeable and useful an Undertaking, as the Printing of this Work, we do allow the Publishing thereof, and recommend the same to all Students of the Law.

In another way this volume was notable. The original manuscript from which it was printed is indicated. It was, the title-page tells us, printed "Solonque les ancient manuscripts ore remanent en les Mains de Sir Jehan Maynard Chevaler, Serjeant de la Ley al sa Tres Excellent Majesty Le Roy Charles le Second." That particular manuscript has been identified. It is now in the British Museum, and its press-mark is Additional Manuscripts, 35094.

Something must be said about the Table of Contents appended to the volume containing the reports of Edward II's reign. The title-page of the volume tells us that the reports are printed according to the ancient manuscripts in the possession of Serjeant Maynard, and that the Table of Matters is the work of the same Serjeant. "Ovesque un perfect Table de Matters en les dits Cases de Temps del' Roy Edward le Second, Colligee per le mesme Serjeant." Let me now quote a few sentences by Maitland, as I cannot state the necessary facts more concisely and pointedly than he has stated them. He says that Maynard's "advanced age[1] and lucrative practice would make it improbable that he did more for the volume than its title-page asserts. He lent a manuscript and furnished a "table of matters." That table—though even it is infamously printed—is the best part of the book. In modern terms we might describe it as a fairly full digest, and, even if it did not bear Maynard's name, we should see that it was the work of one who had diligently read the mediaeval books and had practised the art of 'common-placing.' Now that Maynard did not make this table as an index to the printed book seems certain. Among the Maynard MSS. at Lincoln's Inn there still exists what to all appearance is the original of that table[2]. The contents of this commonplace book, so far as we have examined them, closely agree with the printed table, but whereas the references in the printed table are references to the pages of the printed book, the references in the manuscript are references to years and *placita*....The connexion between the printed table and Maynard's MS. seems to be placed beyond all doubt by the following curious fact, which will illustrate the carelessness with which the publishers of 1678 did their work. Maynard apparently intended to comprise in a single commonplace book the notable matters contained in two different volumes. One of these was a manuscript Year Book of Edward II, the other was Keilwey's Henry VII, which was first printed in 1602: two books, it will be observed, which belong to very different ages. So at the beginning of his notebook Maynard, or his clerk, wrote:

Tabula Annorum *Edwardi* Secundi Regis *etc.* secundum vetus manuscriptum inde. Necnon Relation' de Annis *H.* VII secundum *Kelway*.

Will it be believed that this title, including the mention of Keilwey and Henry VII stands in bold type at the head of the printed table[3]"

at the end of the printed volume of the Year Books of Edward II?

After issuing these hitherto unprinted reports of Edward II, the same printers then went on to reprint the out-of-print volumes of those reports which had been previously printed.

---

[1] Maynard was seventy-five years old at this time. He lived twelve years longer (1602–1690).

[2] Maynard MS. No. 27.

[3] Selden Society's *Year Book Series*, I, pp. xxi–xxii, where much other profitable matter touching the Edward II volume and the table thereto may be read.

They issued nine volumes in 1679[1] and in 1680 the Long Quinto. These ten volumes of 1679 and 1680 were not printed for the three booksellers named in the 1678 volume but were to be sold, so the title-pages tell us, by fifteen different booksellers in London; from which one may perhaps infer that the Atkyns' assignees were the publishers as well as the printers, and the fifteen booksellers only retailing or distributing agents. In this edition the parts or volumes are numbered chronologically, Part I being the years of Edward II and the Exchequer Memoranda of Edward I. The Imprimatur of the second part, containing the first ten years of Edward III, varies from that of the first part, and is instructive as recording the scarceness at the time of the printed editions of the Year Books. It runs:

We, well knowing the grave Use and Benefit of the Year Books and that the scarceness of the same for some years past hath been no small detriment to the Study of the Law, do well approve of the Re-printing: and for the Satisfaction of the Studies and Incouragement of the Undertakers do recommend them to the Students and Professors of the Lawes as a Principal and Essential part of their Study.

Words of practical wisdom, of which it could be wished that those responsible at the time when those old black-letter editions had become practically unintelligible to lawyers and students, responsible not only to see that there was forthcoming a supply of men to serve their country in the profession of the law, but that these were duly qualified so to serve it, had remembered their responsibilities, and had made such provision for a new and, to the modern eye, less repellent edition before, through the difficulties presented in one form and another by the old

---

[1] The 1679 edition of the second half of Henry VI has two title-pages. The first is headed "Syntomotaxia" and refers to the table at the end of the volume, but is preliminary to an Epistle Dedicatory by Robert Barnwal of Gray's Inn, from which the following seems worth extracting: "To the Right Honourable Sir Robert Gardner, Knight, Chief Justice of Ireland—Sir, Among the volumes of the Law that I have read, having found the second part of Henry the Sixt in my opinion worthiest to be heeded, and especially regarded of all those that shall attend the manner and proceeding of Law within the Realm of Ireland; I could not rest satisfied with reading, untill I had drawn such an Index as might serve (if I be not deceived) as well for an Abridgment, as a Table unto the said Volume."

edition, men were repelled from Year Book study, and the Year Books themselves passed for long years into oblivion.

Something must now be said in detail about this edition of the Year Books of 1678–1680. It is in tall folio volumes, and there are eleven of them. Previously the Year Books had all been printed in quarto, a large quarto, form. The volumes of this latest edition were paginated, not foliated, as all the earlier editions had been. The tall folio enabled the printers to get both the recto and the verso sides of the folios of the earlier quarto editions on to one page. The new pagination, therefore, corresponds with the old foliation. At the top of each page is printed a capital A, about half-way down a capital B. The A on page 20, for instance, indicates where the recto of folio 20, according to Tottell's standardized system, begins; the B where the verso of the same folio begins. This edition of eleven parts is now generally known as the Standard Edition, and it is to it that references giving page and other particulars generally apply. With this edition Year Book printing ceased for two hundred years. Let us summarize in very few words what had been done since Machlinia printed his first volume two hundred years before. It is impossible now to say with anything approaching to certainty exactly how many single years and groups of years were separately printed and published during those two centuries, as some of the issues may quite likely have disappeared so entirely that no trace of them is left. But we can say that within that space of time there were at least 445 separately printed issues of years or groups of years. It seems amazing that sources of knowledge which were once spread so widely through our country, and were, obviously, spread so widely only because men valued them and insisted upon having them, should in later days have become so completely neglected and forgotten. This is not, perhaps, the time to assign reasons or to lay the blame for it on these shoulders or those. But the facts remain, account for them how you like. Before passing quite away from this Standard Edition I ought to say that it contains no reports of the twentieth year of Edward II and none at all of Richard II's reign. The Year Books of that reign have never been printed, but in 1584 Richard Bellewe, a barrister of

Lincoln's Inn, edited and published a small volume, measuring only six inches by four and containing 326 pages, in which he brought together the notes of cases heard in Richard II's time, which were scattered throughout the *Abridgements*, compiled and published originally by Statham in 1495, by Fitzherbert originally in 1514 and by Brooke in 1568. Possibly none of the earlier printers had been able to lay his hand on a manuscript authority for that reign, though several are now known. There is one in Cambridge University Library, and there are others in the British Museum and at Lincoln's Inn. The Standard Edition is also incomplete in other ways. Odd years are missing here and there. From the reports of Henry VI, for instance, the years 5, 6, 13, 15, 16, 17, 23 to 26 and 29 are missing. And for one of those missing years certainly, the fifteenth, there is manuscript authority at present available, for I have seen it, in the British Museum. In that same manuscript, it is worth while noting that the reports which the old black-letter editions attribute to the tenth year of Henry VI are attributed to the thirteenth. It would not be difficult, by an examination of the Plea Rolls, to discover which attribution is correct, that of the manuscript in the British Museum or that which the printers presumably followed.

When one considers all this vast output of Year Books, many of them printed and reprinted and reprinted again, one cannot help wondering why no printer thought it worth while printing one of the Eyre Year Books. There were plenty of them in existence. They contained just the same kind of reports as the Year Books which were printed, that is, reports of actions which would have been heard in the Common Bench at Westminster if, by reason of the proclamation of the Eyre, the hearing had not been transferred to the county town in which the Eyre was in session. You cannot distinguish the report of an action heard in the Common Pleas division of a General Eyre from one tried in the Common Bench at Westminster. But in these Year Books of the Eyres you get a large amount of other matter and of reports of other kinds. You have full accounts of all the interesting ceremonies which were observed at the opening of an Eyre, of all the various proclamations published, of the several commissions that were appointed by the Justices for assessing the prices at which food might be sold during the session of the Eyre, for the testing of wine and beer in the county town, for the general regulation of trade throughout the county and for half a dozen other purposes as well. It may be that, as these Eyres had been long dead, all this old ceremonial and procedure had lost its interest for later generations. A knowledge of it had no practical value, and there was no temptation to a sixteenth or seventeenth century printer to be at the expense of printing it. That most interesting procedure by way of bills in Eyre was no longer available, the Eyres themselves being dead, and the printers, knowing, I suppose, nothing and, if possible, caring less about mere legal history, were not concerned with the keeping alive of all the invaluable information as to the origin of the equitable jurisdiction, to mention only one point, which is entombed in the Year Books of the Eyres, and has been forgotten these hundreds of years past. Then, further, these Eyre books contained the only reports of contemporary writs of *quo warranto*, writs which had been withdrawn from the jurisdiction of the Courts at Westminster and were triable only before the Justices of a General Eyre; and these writs abound with all sorts of information as to the privileges and franchises of innumerable ancient manors. Perhaps all this, again, was considered only useless antiquarian lumber; there was nothing in it, or there did not seem to be, that would help a Serjeant in a fight in Court; no suggestion of a useful plea in any of the numerous forms of action which he was daily fighting; no ruling or judgment arising out of any of these actions which he could cite with effect. Anyway, whatever the reason was, no Year Book of an Eyre was published during all that long period of time when Year Books were being turned out in such vast quantities. It was reserved for the Selden Society to print for the first time, about a dozen years ago, the Year Books of a General Eyre, those of the Eyre of Kent of 1313. There are manuscript Year Books of several other Eyres in existence, awaiting an editor, but their chance of finding one in anything like a near future does not at present seem very hopeful.

In this account of the old printed editions of the Year Books some mention ought to be made of the *Abridgements* to which I have just incidentally and casually referred, as they are made up entirely of extracts from the Year Books, and were considered by their compilers, I suppose, to contain the cream of them. These *Abridgements* consist of series of extracts from the Year Books arranged under headings of the various subjects to which the extracts are apposite, upon the law of which they throw some light. The first of these to be printed was Statham's *Abridgement*. It was published by Pynson about 1490. It was probably printed abroad, or if printed in England printed on French paper. The type used is what is called Secretary type, a form of type so unusual in books printed in England that I cannot remember ever having seen one, unless it be that this Statham's *Abridgement* was actually printed in England. There is no date. At the end of a preliminary index is "Per me R. Pynson." No printer's name is given. Nicholas Statham was a Baron of the Exchequer in Edward IV's time. Copies of this *Abridgement* are exceedingly scarce. The first of the three folio volumes of Fitzherbert's *Abridgement* was probably, though not certainly, printed in 1514 and the last in 1516. In the third volume is printed "The price of the whole boke (xl.s.) whych boke conteyneth iii grete volumes." It was probably printed abroad for Wynkyn de Worde. In 1565 Tottell printed an edition of this *Abridgement*. In the Lincoln's Inn copy of this edition some previous owner has written on the title-page "precium 50s." A quarto edition was printed in 1577. Sir Robert Brooke, Chief Justice of the Common Bench, who died in 1558, compiled another lengthy *Abridgement* after the manner of Statham and Fitzherbert. It was printed in 1573, fifteen years after Sir Robert's death, by Tottell. On the title-page of the Lincoln's Inn copy a previous owner has written: "Emptum de Ric. Tottell 18⁰ die Junii 1574, precium 2.6.0." Of these three notable *Abridgements* Fitzherbert's is the best and the one generally used and cited. Fitzherbert, it is clear, had seen manuscript Year Books of earlier date than any which are now known. He has references, which are accepted by competent critics as quite authentic, to Year Books of 12 and 13 Edward I. For other years he has certainly had access to manuscripts which have disappeared, as he now and again gives details which are not to be found in any of the manuscripts now known to us. Somewhat elaborate *Abridgements* of a similar kind with these printed ones were sometimes made by mediaeval lawyers, apparently for their own private use, and have never been printed. There is an exceptionally useful and beautiful manuscript of this kind in the British Museum, its press-mark is Additional MS. 35116, though this is something more and something less than an *Abridgement*. We may receive it in a way amongst the *Abridgements* because its contents are arranged in the fashion followed by the recognized *Abridgements*, but it differs from and excells them in giving in many cases full reports and not merely extracts of a few lines. And the reports it gives of the reign of Edward II are often so different from any other versions we have of the same actions that they are quite uncollatable with them. This manuscript unfortunately covers only some ten years, the last five or six of Edward I and the first four and a half of Edward II. But for those years it is invaluable. I will mention only one other of these manuscript *Abridgements*, and I mention it because it is in Cambridge University Library. The press-mark is Ll. 3. 1. It is a volume of nearly six hundred folios, or double that number of pages. Its contents are arranged alphabetically and extend over the reigns of Edward III, Richard II, Henry IV, Henry V and Henry VI.

With the completion of what we call the Standard Edition in 1680 the curtain fell upon Year Book printing, and was not lifted again until 1866 when Mr Horwood published the first volume of Year Book reports in accordance with the recommendation made by the Select Committee in June, 1800, of which I told you in my first lecture. This first volume gave us the reports of the twentieth and twenty-first years of Edward I. It was followed by reports of the later years. On Mr Horwood's death, Mr Pike took up the work and completed in successive volumes the very limited programme to which the Master of the Rolls had restricted the editors. The original recommendation of the Select Committee was that "the Series of Year Books from Edward I to Henry VIII be completed by printing those hitherto unpublished...and also by reprinting the rest from more correct copies"; a recommendation which, if it had been carried out, would have given us a good working edition of the whole series of Year Books. This handsome programme was cut down in practice to the editing of the unpublished Year Books of Edward I and to the filling up, from hitherto unedited manuscripts, the gap existing in the black-letter editions between the tenth and seventeenth years of Edward III, and between the eighteenth and twenty-first years of the same reign, and the re-editing and re-publishing of the seventeenth and eighteenth years. That is all the assistance which the Government has ever given for the encouragement of Year Book study by the presentation in a reasonably intelligible and readable form of those treasures of our national literature of the multifarious contents of which I tried to give you some short review in my first lecture; of those books which, my Lord Bacon has said it, contain the substance and history of the Common Law of England; all that it has done, all that it gives us any hope that it will do, for the bringing forth of that "new and worthy edition of the Year Books undertaken as a national enterprise" for which Maitland called twenty years ago[1].

But there is more that must be said about the volumes of the Year Books which were edited and published by Horwood and Pike than the mere recapitulation of the years of Edward I and Edward III which they covered. It is impossible to make any comparison between them and the old black-letter editions. In Horwood's volumes we get for the first time a really scholarly and usable edition of the Year Books which they reproduced. The text has been fully expanded and no longer appears in the puzzling abbreviated French of the old editions; and a translation was printed opposite the text, a most obvious necessity if the reports were ever to become of use to those who were not expert in understanding the Anglo-Norman of the original. Then there were instructive Introductions, sufficient indices and useful explanatory notes. Pike's methods were an improvement even upon Horwood's. He introduced the admirable innovation of supplementing and illustrating, wherever he found it possible,

[1] *Year Books*, I, p. xxxii (Selden Society). I have already quoted what Lord Bacon said on this matter as far back as 1614 (p. 4 above).

the report in the Year Book by the corresponding record in the Plea Roll. The report and the record are mutually interpretative of each other, and neither is complete without the other. Pike's last volume was published in 1911. Some eight or nine years before this date the Selden Society, founded, largely by Maitland's efforts, to encourage the study and advance the knowledge of the history of English law, enabled Maitland to do something towards the realization of what was one of the dearest desires of his life, the editing and publication of the Year Books. The Society determined to begin its work on the Year Books with a new and fair edition of those of Edward II. Maitland himself was the first editor. The first volume of the Series was published in 1903, and was followed at intervals by three other volumes, also edited by Maitland. I shall not presume to say more about these volumes and the editing of them than that they fully reached the standard of Maitland's best work, the standard of absolute excellence. Since then the Selden Society has published twelve other volumes of Year Books, including those of the Eyre of Kent of 1313. It has also published a volume dealing specially with those Bills in Eyre to which I have referred; a volume which was almost a necessary supplement to the volumes of the Year Books of the Eyre. The Society, now the only body or organization of any kind that is concerning itself with the editing and publication of Year Books, is still forging its way ahead through waters and weather that have not of late years always allowed it to see its course far ahead. But the prospects are in some ways clearer than they were, and the Society hopes, with some confidence, that it may be able to continue, slowly though it may have to be for the present, its publication of the Year Books of Edward II. Still, if it is to complete this section of its work within a time to which any of us can hopefully look forward, it is essential that its roll of membership should be largely increased.

IV

THE YEAR BOOKS AS A TREASURE-HOUSE
OF LEARNING

A WRITER in the *Spectator*[1], speaking of the Year Books, said that these books "are profoundly interesting, whether to the historian or the lawyer or the student of human nature. One never knows what they will contain besides the legal technicalities which they were designed to preserve." One never knows what they will contain! That writer had to that extent gauged the Year Books. That is really one of their charms. You never know what you are going to find in them, but you are quite certain that you are going to find many a thing outside "the legal technicalities which they were designed to preserve," technicalities which are interesting enough indeed to the lawyer and the student of legal history, but are not, perhaps, very attractive to the general student of social history, of the manners and customs and ways of thinking of mediaeval England. There is no end to the variety, to the unexpectedness of the contents of the Year Books. They are scarcely, for instance, the place where anyone would seek for information about the grafting of apple-trees in the fourteenth century. Yet you will find something for your learning in them about even such an unlikely subject as that[2]. You will come across quaint stories about all sorts and conditions of people and all sorts of things; how, for instance, one man got himself well-dowered with land because he gave Henry II a good dinner when he badly wanted one[3]; how another, in Edward II's reign, lost his office as Warden of the Tower of London because he allowed the Queen's bed-chamber to get into such a bad condition that the rain came in and fell upon her while she was in bed giving birth to a princess[4]. You

---

[1] 27th January, 1923.
[2] 13–14 Edward III, p. 303, case 38 (Rolls Series).
[3] Year Books, 20–21 Edward I (Rolls Series), p. 395.
[4] "Iohannes de Crombewelle...a Constabularia Turris predictae amotus eo quod male custodiebat domos Turris et quia pluviebat super lectum Reginae Angliae puellam nomine Iohannam parturientis ibidem." Eyre of 14 Edward II. *Liber Costumarum* (Rolls Series), 12, II (I), p. 409.

get stories like these; you get valuable scraps of historical fact, of literary history, which the formal chroniclers have failed to record, which industrious editors, seeking elsewhere, have failed to discover. You hear of trades and occupations which have long been obsolete, the very names of some of which are meaningless to us now; details, in short, of every phase and aspect of mediaeval life in England which survive nowhere else. I said, in my first lecture, that there was no question about life in mediaeval England which the Year Books intelligently questioned will not answer. I repeat that again in my last lecture. And I will repeat also that observation of Maitland's, which he made very seriously out of his abundant knowledge of the contents of such Year Books as he had carefully studied, of his sure inference of the contents of such others as time was not given him to study as fully—for it brings into sharp focus the essential value of the Year Books. "It will some day seem a wonderful thing that men once thought that they could write the history of mediaeval England without using the Year Books[1]." If you take that one sentence away with you and realize all that it means, these lectures will not have been without their use.

In my first lecture I gave you some gleanings, gathered more or less at haphazard from the Year Books, of all kinds, but all with their own peculiar interest, all suggestive of lines of thought to the student of mediaeval England from this or that point of view, and there are many points of view from which you can study mediaeval England. Here I want to be more particular, more technical perhaps. Ever since men began to study the history of our law and to write it down for the information of contemporary and future students they have naturally been much exercised about the origin and history of the equitable side of it. For six hundred years and more the most valuable information, information which seems to take us right back to its very origin, was lying in the manuscript Year Books of the Eyres for all men to see, but because no one, I suppose, for hundreds of years had thought of reading these manuscripts and because none of our early printers had thought it worth while to print one of these books of the Eyres, this information lay unknown in our libraries, and continued to lie unknown till

---

[1] *Year Book Series* (Selden Society), I, p. xx.

ten or a dozen years ago when an Eyre Year Book, that of the
Eyre of Kent of 1313, was edited and printed for the first time.
From that Year Book we learned for the first time of an equitable
procedure by what the men of the time called Bills in Eyre, a
procedure which seems the very starting-point of our English
system of Equity. If half a dozen Eyre Year Books had been
edited and that addition to our knowledge had been the only
result, I think that it would have been quite worth while editing
those half a dozen books. I cannot here discuss the full value to
legal history of the disentombment of this long-buried and
entirely forgotten procedure. It has been discussed already by
various writers in various places[1] and I need not say anything
more about it here than just again remind you that it is an
important example of the value of Year Book study to scholarship, which is the particular point of view from which I am
now asking you to consider the Year Books. I want to make
a little digression here and to say something parenthetically,
though it is quite apposite. I said above that I supposed
that no one for centuries past had thought of reading the
manuscript Year Books of the Eyres. Students of the first
book of Coke's *Institutes*, the book we call *Coke upon Littleton*,
if they happen to remember a certain passage in that book
wherein Coke impresses upon his readers the importance and
necessity of reading the Year Books not only in the printed
editions but also in the original manuscripts, may feel inclined
to correct me and say "What about Coke?" I will anticipate
the question. What about Coke? Not every teacher carries out
his own precepts. I think that there has been a growing suspicion
of recent years that Coke's knowledge of the Year Books was
practically confined to what he found in the *Abridgements*. I
have reminded you, if you needed reminding, that he speaks
of the importance of reading the original manuscripts. Exactly
what he says is this—you will find it on page 293 *a* of the first
book of the *Institutes*: "Hereby it also appeareth how necessary
it is to read records and pleas reported or recorded though they
were never printed"; and he says this, apparently, to give force
to his correction of a statement by Littleton, a mistake which he
supposes Littleton would not have made if he had read the

---

[1] *E.g.* Holdsworth, *History of English Law* (3rd ed.), II, pp. 336–344.

manuscript Year Books of the Eyres. Littleton's statement is that a certain ruling was made at an Eyre of Nottingham. Coke corrects Littleton and says that the ruling was made at an Eyre of Northampton and not at an Eyre of Nottingham. Thinking it not improbable that Coke had obtained his information from Fitzherbert's *Abridgement*, I turned up the apposite heading in that book and soon found a note of the ruling mentioned by Littleton. In the margin was Fitzherbert's note, that the ruling was given at the Eyre of Northampton, thus supporting Coke. I did not feel quite satisfied, and I looked up the manuscript Year Books of the Eyres both of Northampton and Nottingham. In the book of the Eyre of Northampton, where both Fitzherbert and Coke say that this particular ruling was given, I could find no reference to it at all. In the Year Book of the Eyre of Nottingham, where Littleton says that it was given, I found it fully set out. The inference seems plain. Coke knew nothing about it but what he had read in Fitzherbert. He had not read the original Year Book. Fitzherbert, of course, had read it. He could not have obtained his information from any other source. But he had made the easily made slip of writing Northampton for Nottingham. This is a little story which has not been told before. The moral of it seems to be that some knowledge of the original Year Books is not only profitable but necessary, especially when you set out to correct Littleton. If there is anyone who is contemplating a new edition of the First Book of the *Institutes*, he, or she, may usefully bear this little story in mind; it may, at any rate, provide matter for an interesting footnote. Now I will resume the direct thread of my present observations on the value of the Year Books to students of legal history. I have spoken of the Bills in Eyre and the light they cast upon the origin of equity. Let us consider next a revelation by the Year Books which will probably give legal historians and teachers of mediaeval law reason for revising opinions which have been generally held and taught for centuries past as to the effect of the well-known Statute *de donis condicionalibus*. Before the promulgation of this statute lands given to a man and the heirs of his body were, by a somewhat casuistical process of reasoning, alienable upon the birth of an heir to the donee. This, of course, was not the intention of the donor, who, it may be supposed, was hoping that he was providing for the comfortable maintenance of his heirs for all time to come. For this very obvious reason, set out in the Statute, it seemed desirable that this power of alienating settled lands upon the birth of an heir to the first beneficiary should be taken away; and the Statute has been undoubtedly held by all lawyers and legal historians to have restrained the alienation of land held in tail, until the ingenious method of a feigned recovery, invented many years later, practically made waste paper of it. But the Year Books throw an entirely fresh light upon the matter, a light that is certainly not over clear, a light that leaves the eyes that are trying to see things as they actually were a little perplexed and confused. The Statute, as I have said, has been held to have restrained alienation absolutely and unconditionally. Chief Justice Bereford, however, in 5 Edward II, ruled that by the actual words of the Statute the original feoffee only was restrained from alienation, that there was no restraint imposed by them on his heir, who was left free to alienate when he succeeded. How, then, did this belief in a perpetual restraint arise in later minds? It arose in great part, no doubt, because no clear knowledge of what the Year Books taught on the matter survived, and in part, probably, from a very important provision which Bereford thought fit to read into the Statute, a provision which it certainly did not contain, a provision which cannot, by any ingenuity whatever, be inferred from anything it does contain. Bereford[1] affected to know, I do not presume to say that he had not private information to that effect, that the makers of the Statute meant to restrain not only the original feoffee, which was all that the words of the Statute as it actually stood did, but to bind also his issue until the fourth degree; and he straightway proceeded to give effect to this non-existent provision, because, he said, though it did not exist it was intended to exist, and only did not exist because of the draftsman's carelessness in omitting it. I have never been able to discover any authority for Bereford's statement. However, he undoubtedly acted upon his own theory, and construed the Statute to restrain alienation until the fourth generation had been reached, and gave effect to that

[1] He seems to have been first summoned to Parliament as a Justice in 1295.

construction. It takes a long time to see four generations through, and one is not over certain when first the procedure by feigned recoveries began to make waste paper of the whole Statute, and it may well be that it was this seemingly arbitrary action by Bereford with its consequent long restraint upon alienation which gave rise to the opinion that has undoubtedly been long held that the Statute intended to restrain alienation absolutely and for all time. Take next for your consideration in this connexion the history of the gradual development of the judicial construction of the seventh section of the Statute of Gloucester. This section, as it stands, was apparently intended to be used only for the recovery of alienated tenements held in dower. It was very soon made to extend to the recovery of alienated tenements held by the curtesy, and as the curtesy might be looked upon as being in some way an inverted kind of dower, the extension seems a quite natural one. By and by Bereford took the section into his consideration, and again he professed to know that the section was meant to cover a great many things which, as it actually stood, it did not cover; and the end of the story of the section's development was that though it appears to have been originally intended to be used for the recovery of alienated tenements held in dower, and for the recovery of these only by those claimants who were able to use certain named writs, it was ultimately made available for the recovery of estates tail by anyone able to use any writ at all, whether a possessory writ or a writ of right, that could be adapted to the purpose[1].

I must touch upon only one matter more in connexion with legal history if I can to keep this lecture within reasonable limits

---

[1] It is now clearly settled law (Hawkins, *Pleas of the Crown*, b. 1, c. 62, s. 1) that no words, whatever their nature may be, will constitute an assault. As a matter of historical interest, and not to overburden my text, I append in a note the report of a case (27 Edward III) where words alone were held to constitute an assault: "Un Collector de la xv dun ville suit pour le Roy et pour luy devers certeins persons de ce qe al temps qe il fut en collectant les deniers du Roy il luy assailit et batit etc. et par force de cele menasse luy enchasa hors de la ville. Que plederent rien culpables trove fuit etc. qe en faisant son office ils luy rebuquerent de mauvais paroles issint qe per cause de cele il nosa demeurer en la ville mais en droit de batterie de rien culpables. Et parce qe trouve fut qe ils luy avoit rebuque etc. et entant il auoit fait assaut et agarde fut qe il recouvre ses damages taxes per lenquest a C.s. Quaere si le Roy neut este partie etc." *Lib. Ass.* (27 Edward III), p. 134, case 11.

of time, but it is an important one, not only important in itself, but important in that it resulted, though by slow degrees, in the common law of the realm winning a supremacy over the foreign canon law. You know that questions involving legitimacy or illegitimacy of birth were reserved for determination by the Bishops' Courts. The moment a plea of illegitimacy was raised in the King's Courts in bar of a plaintiff's claim to recover settled land or to eject from them an alleged illegitimate tenant, and such pleas were being continually made, the jurisdiction of the lay court was stayed. In those mediaeval days, one gathers, it much more frequently happened than it does to-day, that the eldest son of a landowner was born before the marriage of his parents. Sometimes such a son was allowed to succeed his father without objection. Often he was not; and the second son, born within wedlock, promptly brought an action to eject him and to recover the family estate for himself. Sometimes the second son took possession immediately upon his father's death, and the eldest son, born out of wedlock, brought his action for recovery, on the ground that he was his father's eldest son and heir. Illegitimacy was, of course, always pleaded on the one side or the other; and the Justices of the King's Court had no option but to send the question for determination to the Bishop. The Bishop administered canon law. The canon law said that a son born before the marriage of his parents was legitimatized by their subsequent marriage. The common law of the realm, as declared "with one voice" by the Earls and Barons at Merton, said emphatically that a son born before the marriage of his parents was incapable of succeeding. The two systems of law were in direct conflict. An elder brother, born before the marriage of his parents, has taken possession of the family estate. His younger brother, born within wedlock, brings his action to recover them. "You are illegitimate," he says to his brother, "and you are not capable of succeeding to the estate." "I am legitimate," the elder brother replies; "ask the Bishop." And the Court must ask the Bishop. And it knows perfectly well what the Bishop will say; that he will say that the elder son is legitimate. And the King's Court is bound to accept what the Bishop says and to give effect to it: to maintain the elder son, born out of wedlock, in possession of the family estate, to which the common law of the realm says that he is incapable of succeeding, to the exclusion of the second son, born within wedlock, whom the common law of the realm declares to be the lawful heir, entitled to possession. The whole thing was against the conscience of the King's Justices, and, one would suppose, against the conscience of the country generally. But for long years there seemed no help for it, no way out of the difficulty. It would have been impolitic, impossible perhaps, to have deprived the ecclesiastical courts of their jurisdiction. But it became increasingly evident that such a state of things could not be allowed to continue indefinitely. Could no practicable way be found out of the difficulty? Was it, after all, necessary to plead illegitimacy or legitimacy in just that straightforward, naked form? Could you not get to the same end by a rather more roundabout path? Suppose that instead of saying bluntly that John was illegitimate, you said merely that he was born before the marriage of his parents, and kept quite silent about illegitimacy. Whether John was or was not born before the marriage of his parents was a quite simple question of fact, requiring no theological knowledge or ecclesiastical authority to determine; one which a lay jury was quite competent to try. The lay jury tries it and finds, as a matter of fact, that John was born before the marriage of his parents. It, also, discreetly says nothing about legitimacy or illegitimacy. The Court now deals with the jury's finding of a matter of fact. The jury has found that John was born before the marriage of his parents; by the common law of the realm, the Court says, one who is born before the marriage of his parents is incapable of succeeding. From first to last no word has been said of legitimacy or illegitimacy; no infringement of ecclesiastical jurisdiction has been made; but at last justice has been done, and the common law of the realm has won its way over the foreign canon law. It all seems very simple when you hold the key of the puzzle, but it took a long time and much arguing and theorizing before the pattern of that key was devised and the key itself made and fitted into the lock. I do not know where, outside our old Year Books, you will find the full story of the devising of that key, and the story of the devising of that key is surely legal history[1].

As to the value and importance of the Year Books to the lawyer and the student of law as distinct from the legal historian —if, indeed, we can draw any sharp distinction between law and legal history—there is surely no need to show that formally or at any length. It will be enough to cite Lord Bacon—whom I have already quoted to you[2]—and Coke in proof. Lord Bacon has told us that the common law of England consisteth in the series and succession of judicial acts from time to time which have been set out in the books which we term Year Books. Coke has told us that "the learned Sages of the law doe found their judgment upon legal reason and judicial President; the one they find in our bokes of yeares and termes, the other out of records formerly examined and allowed[3]." I need not press the point further. The importance to the lawyer of a knowledge of the Year Books is too obvious, when once we know what they contain, to need further words to set it out.

The student of the social customs of the Middle Age in England, of mediaeval life in England generally; what is there in the Year Books that will help him to a better knowledge, a fuller understanding of it? How do the Year Books illustrate all this? The chief difficulty I have in answering this question is to keep myself within reasonable limits. There is material enough to the point available for more than a whole lecture, for a course of lectures, indeed. The Year Books throw a light upon each and every side of mediaeval life, bringing into distinctness details of all kinds which I do not know that you will find set out with anything like the same particularity and stated with the same certificate of authority anywhere else. Most of the things which I am going to tell you have nothing to do with law, but of the circumstances and surroundings in which our mediaeval forefathers lived, of what they ate and drank; on what sort of terms they lived with their neighbours, and so on; some knowledge of which is absolutely necessary if we would know

[1] In what goes immediately before I have borrowed, necessarily, somewhat from a lecture by me in the University of London at a little earlier date on Chief Justice Sir William Bereford.

[2] Pp. 4, 81 above.   [3] Introduction to his *Boke of Entries*.

what life in mediaeval England was like; knowledge which cannot be obtained in such fulness and wideness from any other source. I spoke incidentally in my first lecture of corrodies, which I explained were grants of board and lodging in religious houses. They were made to all sorts and conditions of men, from those who had been in the higher classes of the King's personal service to very poor people who were quite without means of their own. Mention of grants of these corrodies occurs frequently in the Year Books. Exactly what is granted in the way of lodging and food is often specifically set out, and these details provide us with valuable and authoritative information as to the style of living, of the daily quantity and nature of the food and drink which was considered suitable and necessary for representatives of the different sections of mediaeval society in England. I have written elsewhere[1] at some length of these corrodies and of the information with which they supply us, and I will not now repeat what I have already said. The working man or small tenant of the Middle Age was often concerned with how he was going to live when he had passed the time of life when he could do any active work for his own maintenance and when he had no one to whom he could look to keep him during his years of inefficiency. There were no old age pensions in those days, there was no system of insurance. The individual man must make for himself what best arrangement he could. And what does the man who had scraped together some small amount of ready money or had managed to buy some little tenement do in these circumstances? He went to some man of more substance than himself and made over to him his scanty savings or scrap of land in return for a promise of such bare food and lodging as he could bargain for for the rest of his life. He had no security that the man with whom he made his bargain would always himself be in a position to carry it out; no security that even if he could he would. And often, I am afraid, these poor men were turned out of the homes which they thought they had secured for the rest of their lives to beg their bread as best they could. But of that, too, I have written elsewhere[2], and I do not want

[1] *The Year Books* (Cambridge University Press), pp. 70–73.
[2] *Bills in Eyre* (Selden Society), pp. lv, lvi.

to take up too much of the limited time which remains to me
by repeating what I have said before. I am at present engaged
in showing to you the importance of the Year Books to the student
of the general social life of the Middle Age in England, and I
must content myself with just pointing out to you some of the
many phases of that life upon which our old Year Books cast
a clear light. When a man of to-day, who owns a single house
or thousands of acres of land, wants to raise money for some
immediate need, he goes to someone who is able and willing to
lend him the money he needs and gives him, by way of security
for its repayment, a mortgage on his land. By the terms of that
mortgage he undertakes to pay a certain amount of interest
regularly and to repay the whole sum lent either at a definite
date or after a certain notice. Our mediaeval ancestors who
needed ready money generally went about matters in a quite
different way, they adopted a converse method. Instead of the
borrower remaining in possession of his land, as he does to-day
until he makes default in the covenants of his mortgage, the
mediaeval borrower at once put the lender of the money into
possession of his land, taking from him a promise, sometimes in
writing and sometimes, apparently, a merely verbal one, that he
would re-convey the land to him on his repayment of the money
lent. This system often led to much hardship, to much in-
equity. The lender of the money found himself very comfortable
and contented where he was. He preferred to retain the land
to giving it up and getting back the money he had lent. The land,
he would argue, had been conveyed to him absolutely, as indeed
it had been; anything else that had been said or written afterwards was a quite different matter. It might give the borrower
some ground, perhaps, on which he might bring an action for
breach of covenant for which he would possibly be entitled to
damages, but it would not entitle him to recover the land; and
this, I am afraid, was passably good law in those days, and the
owner would never get his land back again. The present system
and law of mortgage was a long time in getting itself evolved and
settled. In those days usury was forbidden, but nevertheless it
seems to have been practised, and the rate of interest sometimes
charged does not look small even when compared with the rate

which we gather from the newspapers is not infrequently charged by the modern money-lender. Let me tell you very briefly the story of Thomas Trie of Ludlow as set out in an unprinted Year Book of the Shropshire Eyre of 1292[1]. In 1272 Thomas wanted to borrow twenty shillings for a short time. He found a Jew who was willing to lend it to him upon the condition that Thomas should find a substantial guarantor for the repayment of thirty shillings at the end of seven weeks. This works out at the rate of about 375 per cent. per annum. Thomas found a suitable guarantor, but this guarantor would only guarantee Thomas upon the condition that Thomas would put him in possession of a certain house. Thomas put him in possession and went back to the Jew with his guarantee; and the Jew thereupon gave him seven shillings by way of instalment, and Thomas never received any more than that amount, though the Jew kept the guarantor's bond for the repayment of the full thirty shillings. At the end of the seven weeks the Jew went to the guarantor with the bond and claimed the thirty shillings. The guarantor parlied and bargained with him and succeeded in getting his bond back on the payment of fifteen shillings, which works out at about 800 per cent. per annum. Thomas then went to his guarantor and wanted to redeem his house by the repayment to him of the fifteen shillings he had paid to the Jew. The guarantor refused to give up possession unless Thomas paid him twenty-four shillings. Thomas did not want to lose his house and managed to raise the twenty-four shillings somewhere and paid them to his guarantor. But even then he did not get his house back, and never at any time afterwards did he get it back; and what the rate of interest was which he finally paid for his loan of seven shillings I will leave you to calculate for yourselves. Of all sorts of what we may call social happenings we get records in these old books, and many of them certainly do not incline us to suppose that the course of mediaeval life in England was a very placid one, that it altogether deserved that appellation of "merry" which has not infrequently of later years been conferred upon it. I can give you only a very few examples. We read, for instance, of the wife of a lord

[1] Cf. *Bills in Eyre*, pp. lvii and 15.

of a manor, a lady who might be supposed to set something like a standard of manners for the neighbourhood, calling in at a neighbouring house, attacking the mistress of it, felling her to the ground, and then battering her head with stones until she destroyed the poor woman's hearing[1]. We read of all sorts of assaults, most murderous assaults, some of them, made upon helpless women in the presence of a crowd of bystanders, not one of whom seems to have raised a finger in their protection. We seldom or never read of anything which makes for the happiness of life, which tends to the credit of anyone. But those are the things which as a rule keep themselves out of legal records; and we must not suppose, because we read of so much savagery, especially in those old Year Books of the Eyres, which, with one exception, have never been printed, that there were no pleasant places, no happy people, living happily in mediaeval England. But you certainly cannot get anything like a full picture of life in England in those times without the Year Books. There is no such record of it anywhere else.

What next shall I dig out of these old books in this connexion? Something I ought to say, perhaps, about the custom of Sanctuary, for it was a characteristic part of mediaeval English life leading sometimes to roadside scenes of tragedy, the like of which we can hardly imagine to-day. If a criminal could get himself inside a church before he was arrested, he might stay there for forty days unmolested and might be supplied with food and drink; every precaution, of course, being taken that he did not escape. At the end of the forty days any further supply of food was forbidden, and starvation faced the refugee. But if he chose, as I suppose that he always in the end did choose, to swear that he would make his way to such port as was assigned to him and there leave the country, he was allowed to do so. But he must not leave the highway; he must not deviate from the straight road. If he did his life was at anyone's mercy; and we have gruesome stories of these strayers from the high road being seized and murdered, their heads cut off there and then maybe, just where they were caught. Let me notice next

[1] *Bills in Eyre*, pp. lii and 66.

the old trial by battle. In certain matters, you will remember, the final issue was determined by a fight between champions representing the opposing litigants. The result of this fight, a fight to the death it might be, between these representative champions, determined in mediaeval eyes and according to mediaeval law the real right and wrong as to the matter in issue. If the plaintiff's champion won, the plaintiff won his action and all that he was seeking to obtain. If the defendant's champion won, then the plaintiff lost his action. Several of our old Year Books give us various particulars of the preliminaries to these trials by battle; of the presentation to the Court of the respective champions, of their examination by the Justices and so on. Some of these notices occur in Year Books which have been printed, others occur in unprinted ones. In an unprinted Year Book in Lincoln's Inn of the Northamptonshire Eyre of 3 Edward III are some quaint details which are set out with a fulness which I do not remember to have seen elsewhere, which may be worth telling here. We are in Court. The Justices are sitting on the Bench. Just below them is the clerk's table. The two champions are brought in. One of them is told to stand at one end of the table, the other at the other end. The Justices looked at their feet to see whether they had taken their boots off, and it was found that they had done so. I do not feel quite sure of the meaning of this piece of ritual. Then Chief Justice Scrope told the champions to hand their gloves to him, and the champions did so, on their knees. When the Chief Justice got hold of the gloves he appears to have turned them inside out, and assured himself that there was a penny stowed away at the end of each of the fingers, fivepence in all, in each of the gloves, one glove of each champion. Then he put the pennies back into the gloves and returned gloves and pennies to the champions. Then the champions exchanged gloves with each other for a moment, and then each resumed possession of his own. The gloves were then again handed to the Chief Justice who at once returned them to their respective owners. All this ritual meant something definite, I suppose, but what it did mean is not as yet clear to me. But we do gather what the pennies were for. The Chief Justice made a little speech to the opposing litigants, in the course of which he told them to keep their respective champions well away from each other until they met on the field. Then he bade the defendant take his champion to a church and the plaintiff take his to another, and there the two champions were to offer the five pennies in their gloves in honour of the five wounds of God, that God might give the victory to him that had the right. The report from which I have extracted these details is a report of an action to determine the right to the advowson of a church. It seems to throw a curious light upon the mentality of our ancestors, who apparently considered that the best way to settle who should make provision for the cure of souls in a certain parish was to set two of the people whose souls were in question to do their best to batter those souls out of each other's bodies and to set them beyond the cure or care of anyone.

The liability to jury service has been much extended lately. It will probably be a source of satisfaction to the women, at any rate, who are now called upon to serve to know that certain unpleasant methods of dealing with jurors of which we read in the Year Books are not now likely to fall within their own experience. Dissentient jurors were occasionally sent to prison to punish their obstinacy[1], and to teach them to be more conformable in the future. Juries which were hopelessly divided in opinion were locked up indefinitely without food or drink. "Good people," said Stanton J. to such a jury, "you cannot agree? Go, put them in a house till Monday, and let them not eat or drink." This had the desired effect. The report goes on: "on the same day about vesper time they agreed[2]." A jury was "commanded to abide in one chamber, without eating or drinking, until they agreed. And on the morrow they had agreed[3]." They might be dragged about in carts at the tail of the Justices from assize-town to assize-town until they could make up their minds[4]. If the Justices had gone home to dine and did not want

---

[1] "Et pur ceo qe lun de la Iure auoit tarie ses compagnions par un iour et un nuit sans assenter a eux et cel sans resoun fuit agarde qil demurrast en le Flete. Et puis fuit il lesse a mainprise tanque la Court soyt avise ceo quil vout faire de luy." *Lib. Ass.*; 9 Edward III, p. 20, case 35. And see *The General Eyre*, pp. 87–88; and Egerton MS. (British Museum), fo. 210 d.

[2] *Year Book Series* (Selden Society), IV, p. 188.

[3] 20 (1) Edward III (Rolls Series), p. 488.

[4] 19 Edward III (Rolls Series), p. 185.

to come all the way back to Court to receive a verdict, the jurors were taken to some convenient place near at hand, a church, for example, and there the Justices received their verdict[1]. Between retiring to consider his verdict and delivering that verdict a juror had to be very careful what he did; or, rather, had to be very careful that he did nothing at all but consider his immediate business. To eat or drink aught would not only get him into serious trouble with the Court if it came to its cognizance, but would, as likely as not, invalidate the verdict when given. Even to put on an overcoat before delivering his verdict was a serious offence, as a certain Sir John Spek learned to his hurt. Before returning into Court he had taken his coat[2] from his servant who was holding it and had put it on. The officers of the Court who had the jury in charge protested against this breach of rule and reported it to the Court, who committed Sir John to the Fleet prison, from which he was released only on paying a fine of forty shillings[3]. But sometimes the Court was a little more considerate of human frailties. In 14 Henry VII a jury was trying a case in the Exchequer Chamber. After they had been sworn, and while the parties were giving evidence, a violent thunderstorm broke out and so frightened some of the jurors that they left the Court for what they considered some safer place, without the leave of the Justices. When they came back they delivered their verdict. I gather from the report that their unwarranted departure had not been noticed, and so I infer that the violence of the storm had frightened the whole Court into a temporary adjournment; and when the facts were made known to the Court they quashed the verdict, but do not seem to have punished the fugitive jurors[4]. On the other hand, there were recognized reasons for exemption from jury service which it would be unavailing to plead to-day. We have, for instance, cases reported in the Year Books of Henry IV and Henry VI[5]

[1] 19 Edward III (Rolls Series), p. 185.
[2] "Armulansam duplicatam."
[3] *Liber Intrationum*, fo. clxxv.
[4] "Les Jurors furent esleus tries et jures et quand les parties furent monstrants lour evidence la avient tiel tempest de thunder et de pluye qe ascuns des Jurors departerent sans conge des Justices." Year Books, Tr. 14 Henry VII, p. 29, case 4; continued Hil. 15 Henry VII, p. 1, case 2.
[5] Year Books, Hil. 2 Henry IV, p. 15 and Easter 19 Henry VI, p. 66, case 16.

where jurors were challenged because they were godfathers of one or other of the parties to the action. "But," adds the reporter in 2 Henry IV, "it was not so considered in earlier times, and such a challenge has not always been allowable." We say to-day that the law is no respecter of persons, but that does not, according to the Year Books, appear always to have been the theory. In a case heard in 3 Henry VI, counsel for one of the parties prayed that a certain person might be brought into Court to be examined. This was a proposal that seems to have somewhat shocked Chief Justice Cockayne. "He is a Peer of the Realm," he expostulated, "and it would not be seemly to make him come here; you might, for like reason, make any or every Duke or Earl in England come here": and counsel answered: "Why not, Sir? Our law applies to everybody. The Statute subjects everyone to it, be he high or low." But the Chief Justice would not agree. The law, he said, had a different application to different classes of people; there was a difference in the way it applied to a lord or a lady and to common people. The reporter has added: "Quere: what is the difference[1]?" In this connexion I may, not inappositely, mention the case of one "Wingfield Esquier" who was remanded to gaol in 21 Edward IV as being concerned in a case of homicide. The Justices refused to commit him to Newgate—"it is too sordid a prison for him who is a gentleman and an Esquire of the King's Household"— and they sent him to the Fleet[2].

Fortescue, in his *De laudibus legum Angliae*, writes:

I would ye should know that the Justices of Englande sit not in the King's courts above iij. houres in a day, that is to say, from viij of the clock in the forenoone til xi, complete. In the afternoones those

---

[1] Year Books, Trin. 3 Henry VI, p. 45, case 5.

[2] "Et pur ceo qe le Marshal de Bannk le Roy avoit espose la soer cely appelle il fuit commande al Flete et les Justices disont qe ils ne voillent lui committer al N[ewgate] pur ceo qe il est trop vile prison pur luy car il est Gentle homme et Esquier del hostel le Roy.... Et nota qe cel enprisonment ne fuit forsque par discreccion del Court car il fuit lesse a baille deins iij. jours apres. Et un Esquier del hostel le Roy appella *Brandon* qe fuit le nephew le dit *Wingfield* disoit a les Justices pur quoy naura il favor car il ad fait al Roy plus bon service qe ascun dautre party auoit ou puissoit faire. *Hussey* [C.J.K.B.] dit a luy departes del barre ou verament toy serrez ovesque luy, par quei *Brandon* fuist pawn̄ rebuk et departi del barre." Year Books, Mich. 21 Edward IV, p. 71, case 55.

courts are not holden or kept. But the suters then resort to the perusing of their writings and elsewhere consulting with the Serjeants at law and other their counsaylors. Wherefore the Justices, after they have taken their refection, doe passe and bestow all the residue of the day in the study of the lawes, in reading of holy scripture and using other kind of contemplation at their pleasure. So that their life may seem more contemplative than active. And thus doe they lead a quiet life, discharged of all worldly cares and troubles.

Fortescue was Chief Justice of the Common Bench in Henry VI's reign, and is, therefore, presumably, an excellent authority for the procedure of the Common Bench and the Justices in Henry VI's time. But I cannot make what he says fit in with the plain evidence of the Year Books of that time. In the Easter Term of 4 Henry VI, Justice Martyn made this remark in the Common Bench: "It is plainly apparent to me that Rolfe [Rolfe was a Serjeant arguing a case in Court] has been dining well to-day, as it seems to me that he has eaten an error[1]." "Has been dining well to-day." That could not, one thinks, have been said unless the Court had been sitting after dinner, and Fortescue says that the Court did not sit after dinner. I cannot reconcile the authorities, but the evidence of the Year Book is very plain and strong. What have the Year Books to tell us about the observance or non-observance of Sunday in mediaeval England? You will remember that Sir Edward Coke tells us that

in the common law there be *dies juridici* and *dies non juridici*, that the *dies non juridici* are the Lord's days throughout the whole year... and this was the ancient law of England, and extended not only to legal proceedings but to contracts etc.

I am sorry that I must again impugn a recognized authority, but again I cannot make the plain testimony of the Year Books fit in with Coke's statement. In a reported case of the Trinity Term of 15 Edward III, the Abbot of St Albans produced a deed of conveyance—a release, strictly—of land to the Abbey of St Albans executed by the Prior of Bushmead. And this

---

[1] "*Martyn J.* Mes ies voy bien qe *Rolf* ad bien disne cest jour car come me semble il ad mange dun error." Year Books, 4 Henry VI, p. 24, case 11. And it may be worth while adding: "Et puis manger touts les Justices furent a l' Blackfriers pur les materes le Roy encountre le Parlement." Year Books, Mich. 1 Henry VII, p. 3, case 3.

document is dated at Bushmead "in capitulo nostro die dominica proxima post festum sancti Dionysii[1]." This makes it clear, I think, that ecclesiastics of high position in Edward III's time did not agree with Coke that Sundays were *dies non juridici*. That the lawyers of the time did not agree with him may safely be inferred from the fact that no exception was taken to the deed and that it was held to be good in law. We find people who were neither ecclesiastics nor lawyers levying distresses and executing legal documents on Sundays and no objection taken to them on that ground[2]. But in one respect Sunday had, at any rate in certain places, a special sacredness. It was much more expensive to commit crimes on that day than on any other. In Chester, for instance, he who shed blood between Saturday noon and Monday morning had to pay twenty shillings. The cost of doing so at other times was only half that sum. A Sunday burglary cost the burglar four pounds; for the like crime on other days he got off with two pounds; and so on[3]. There seems to have been a good deal of Sunday trading, and I have seen notices of local regulations prohibiting strangers coming in from outside and opening stalls during the time when the faithful parishioners were hearing mass, as it put these latter at a disadvantage compared with those more careless traders who were neglectful of their religious duties. There is good reason to suppose that from the time of Richard I, at any rate, to that of Henry VI, the distinction between Sundays and other days was not very much recognized by either churchmen or laymen. And the Courts, we know, sat not only at Westminster but in the country on Sundays just as upon other days[4]. Amongst other social customs of the time was a fairly prevalent one which could not have added to the amenities of the mediaeval streets, the apparently incorrigible habit of the townspeople of turning

[1] 14 Edward III (Rolls Series), p. lviii.

[2] Some actual instances may be given. Distraints on Sundays are recorded in the Plea Roll of Easter, 8 Edward II (No. 209) on rr. 21 and 24. The latter records a Sunday distraint in 30 Edward I. The same roll (r. 149 *d*) records the execution of a quitclaim on a Sunday in 27 Edward I; and the roll for Trin. 8 Edward II (No. 211), r. 32, records the execution of a bond on a Sunday.

[3] *Borough Customs*, II, p. 46 (Selden Society, vol. XXI).

[4] *Eyre of Kent* (Selden Society), I, p. 1, and *De Banco* Plea Roll, Hil. 8 Edward II (No. 208), r. 212 *d*.

their pigs loose in them, there to wander at their will, picking up what they could. Even in the Middle Age, pigs wandering at will through the narrow streets of the city of London must have been something of a nuisance, and regulations were made from time to time in London and elsewhere prohibiting it under a penalty. A fine was generally imposed for the first transgression. For a second, your pig might be killed at sight, by anyone in some places, in others, by the official pindar. Canterbury tacked on to its own regulations an order that the carcass of a pig killed under these regulations was to be distributed amongst the poor. But I do not think that these regulations and punishments were altogether effective. It was a case of give and take. "You turn a blind eye to my pigs, and I won't see yours. They are picking up a certain amount of food at no cost to anyone; and, after all, they are doing something to clear the streets of garbage[1]."

But "the bird of time has but a little way to flutter, and the bird is on the wing," and I want to say something of the value of the Year Books to the student of our language, to the philologist, the etymologist. And the first reflection that one is prompted to make is one of regret that when thought was being taken for the preparation of the great Oxford Dictionary no one was assigned to examine the Year Books—that no one was so assigned I have on the authority of Dr Bradley[2], the present editor-in-

---

[1] The following writ, of uncertain date, gives an unsavoury picture of mediaeval Oxford: "Rex maiori et balliuis suis Oxonie salutem. Quia ex testimonio accepimus fide digno quod per fimos et fimaria necnon porcarias et frequentem accessum porcorum ac plures alias foeditates que in viis et venellis ville predicte et suburbiis eiusdem existunt aer ibidem in tantum corrumpitur et inficitur quod magistris et scholaribus in eadem commorantibus et aliis ibidem conuersantibus et transeuntibus horror abhominabilis incutitur commoditas salubrioris aeris impeditur status hominum grauiter laeditur alieque intolerabiles incommoditates et quam plurima discrimina ex corruptione huiusmodi peruenire noscuntur in magistrorum et scholarium predictorum et aliorum ibidem conuersantium et transeuntium nocumentum et vite sue periculum manifestum: nos nolentes huiusmodi defectus enormes et intolerabiles ibidem vlterius sustinere vobis precepimus quod omnes vicos et venellos in villa predicta et eius suburbiis de fimis et fimariis ac aliis foeditatibus predictis mundari et mundatos in posterum conseruari sine dilatione aliqua faciatis ne per corruptiones aut foeditates predictas damnum seu periculum aliquibus in vestri defectu eueniat in futuro per quod ad vos tanquam ad mandati nostri contemptores grauiter capere debeamus." *Register of Writs*, fo. 267 *d.*

[2] Whose death since these words were written all scholarship deplores.

chief of the Dictionary. That men should think that they could compile a complete and really comprehensive dictionary of the English language without the Year Books seems every whit as wonderful a thing as Maitland has told us it will seem some day that men thought that they could write the history of mediaeval England without them. But, unfortunately, so it was. The great Dictionary was planned and put together without any reference to the Year Books. I cannot, of course, here and now, go with any detail into the value of the Year Books to the philologist and etymologist. I can only assert it emphatically and call at any rate one witness of unimpeachable authority, the late Prof. Skeat, in support of the assertion. It was only, unfortunately, during the last few months of his life that Skeat's attention was attracted to the Year Books, to that edition of the Year Books of the Eyre of Kent by the Selden Society which I have already mentioned. He told me with lively enthusiasm of what he characterized as startling and important facts which he had already discovered from reading them and had noted for future use. Of a list of words which I had sent him he wrote: "The most extraordinary thing is that your examples of these words are often a great deal earlier and older than those in the *N.E.D.*, which requires much explanation." The explanation, of course, was that the Year Books had not been looked at in the preparation of the Dictionary. It may be worth while telling you, with some detail, just a single example of the value of the Year Books to the philological scholar, all that Skeat read and deduced from one single word on which his eyes had lighted in that particular Year Book, the word *notch*.

After adverting to the comparatively recent examples of the word given in the Oxford Dictionary, he went on:

Yet here we have *noche* already in Anglo-French in 1313. And it *must* have been then in use in English also (of course in connexion with the tally), because the *n* is English; for *a noche* was due to *an oche*; the real Old French word being *oche*. Indeed, the *N.E.D.* does record *oche* in the fifteenth century as a verb; and the substantive from which the verb was derived must already have been known[1].

---

[1] When Prof. Skeat wrote the above no instance of the occurrence of this word was known either to him or to me. I have since then met with it. See *Year Book Series* (Selden Society), XVII, p. xxxvii.

The whole problem is most interesting to the English etymologist. You even have, at p. 35[1], the verb *annocer*, which is probably a substitution for *enoccer*, seeing that the Anglo-French not infrequently substitutes initial *an-* for French *en-*, Latin *in-*. It is difficult to say whether *a-nocer* was derived from the substantive *noche*, or whether (which is quite possible) it means *an-occer*, answering to a Latin *in-occare*, an instance of which, meaning "to harrow in," is given in Lewis and Short's *Latin Dictionary*. *Inoccare* might easily have been taken to mean "to score (land) with a harrow." I daresay we may get further someday. Anyhow, the Anglo-French *nocha* is an undoubted fact.

There I must leave detail, and content myself for the rest of the very short time remaining to me with some general statements, with just a note or two about some individual words as typical of what could have been gathered from the Year Books for the emendation or extension of what is set out in the Dictionary. Take the forms *Latiner* and *Latimer*. The Dictionary says that the meanings of the two forms are quite distinct and invariable; that *Latiner* is, to put it shortly, a Latin scholar, that *Latimer* is an interpreter, and that *Latiner* is never used in that sense. In the Hilary term of 34 Henry VI[2] a case was heard to which a foreigner who could not speak our language was a party. He was allowed to engage the services of an interpreter, and that interpreter is plainly written down as a *Latiner* and not as a *Latimer*. That is an example of a certain emendation that would have been made in the Dictionary if the Year Books had been consulted. Now for an example of a probable extension of the meaning of a word, as given in the Dictionary, about which I myself wrote to Dr Bradley and I think elicited his interest in a certain apposite extract from the *Liber Assisarum* of the second year of Edward III which I sent to him. It reported a case of novel disseisin in the course of which it was said that the agent of the defendant came on to the land in question and cut down the thorn-trees and dug up the ground and made pitfalls, by way of asserting his right to possession. None of the meanings

---

[1] *I.e.* in *Eyre of Kent*, II.

[2] "Choke [C.J.]... en cas qe ascun estranger soit greve qe ne sauoit parler en ceo cas est loial pur chescun homme qe scait parler sa language de estre *Latiner* et monstre le matter a son consel etc." Year Books, Hil. 34 Henry VI, p. 25, case 3.

assigned by the Oxford Dictionary to the word "pitfall," which are the meanings commonly assigned to it to-day, seems to explain the meaning of "pitfall" as used in that old report. It can hardly, in the circumstances, have its present-day meaning, though I am not over ready to suggest the meaning it really carried. And, it may be added, this instance of "pitfall" is sixty years older than the earliest given by the Oxford Dictionary. Then in the Year Books we get now and again passing observations about what one may call linguistic matters which are interesting to us to-day. For instance, it was ruled from the Bench by Chief Justice Hengham in 1304, 32 Edward I[1], that "H" was not a letter, and that consequently it did not matter whether you wrote and, inferentially, whether you said, Hersham or Ersham; that there was no such variance between the two forms as would admit of any objection on the plea of variance being raised on that ground. In 9 Henry VI was again discussing the potency of this same letter. Ought you to write and say "habilem" or "abilem"? Babington J. said that some people in the Chancery—I do not know why the Chancery should have been allowed any special authority in such a question, unless it were that the clerks of the Chancery drafted the writs—said that "habilem" was the proper form, while others said that "abilem" was. "And so," the Judge concluded, "you won't be harmed by spelling it either way or both ways[2]." These are Year Book contributions to the history of the use of our aspirate. In the documents of a case in the fourth year of Henry VI, in 1425, the name of a certain place had been variously written Banester and Benester, and objection founded on this variance was taken. Justice Martyn, however, over-ruled it, and proceeded, in support of his ruling, to deliver an interesting little dissertation on the different pronunciation of words in different parts of England, instancing the different pronunciations prevalent in different parts of the country, "and one," he said, "is just as good as the other[3]." When Mr Samuel Weller the younger was called in the Court of Common Pleas to give evidence in

[1] 32 Edward I (Rolls Series), p. 128.
[2] Year Books, Mich. 9 Henry VI, p. 53, case 37.
[3] Year Books, Mich. 4 Henry VI, p. 6, case 17.

Bardell v. *Pickwick* and was asked by the Judge whether he spelt his name with a "V" or a "W" he might have cited, in support of his answer, that it depended upon the taste and fancy of the speller, the *dictum* of an earlier Judge of that same Court —a *dictum* or ruling that was given in these circumstances. In the ninth year of Henry VI an action was brought to recover £20 secured by a bond. The bond, after the fashion of the time, was in Latin, and the scribe had written *wiginti* instead of the more usual *viginti*. Serjeant Newton argued for the defendant that he could not properly be called on to reply to a bond so drafted, for *wiginti* had no meaning. Paston J., however, did not agree. He said that "W" was nothing more than a couple of "V's" and that it made no matter whether you wrote William or Villiam, which is practically what Mr Weller said. Cottesmore J., who was also on the Bench at the time, met this with something like a flat contradiction:

If (said he) you spell a word with an initial W you pronounce it one way, while if you spell it with an initial V you pronounce it another way. You cannot contend that J. Wise and J. Vise are one and the same person.

Chief Justice Babington, who was presiding, does not appear to have expressed any opinion on the question, and whether any ruling was given as to the validity of a bond by which the obligee had bound himself to pay *wiginti libras* is not apparent from the report[1], which is at any rate of interest as showing that there was a common confusion of "W" and "V" in the early years of Henry VI, or otherwise a trained legal scribe would scarcely have written *wiginti* for *viginti*. One other thing one would like to know is how he pronounced *wiginti*.

---

[1] "En bref de debte *quod reddat xl. l* et lobligatorie escrit fuit *wiginti* ove [*w*]....*Newton*. Nous ne serroms mis a respoundre a ceste obligation: car ceo parole [*wiginti*] nad nul entendement....*Paston*. Lobligation est assez bon car un double [*W*] n'est forsqe ij. sengle [*V*]...et si Willelmus soit escrit [*Villelmus*] par sengle [*V*] uncore lobligacion est assez bon....*Cottesmore.* Mes si un parole soit escrit par double [*W*] il sonne en un maner et si par sengle [*V*] il son en autre maner car [*J. Wise*] et [*J. Vise*] ne peut estre entendu un meme person etc. et issint lobligacion est voide. *Newton.* Nous prioms qe le roule qe sera de recorde soit fait accordant al obligation viz. *wiginti. Babington.* Non pas: car le roule serra accordant al bref et al declaration etc." Year Books, Easter, 9 Henry VI, p. 7, case 15.

Look at these books now for a single moment from the point of view of the historian of literature. Can he learn anything from them? Let me give you a single instance of what he may gather from them. There is a fragment of a ballad, or what is supposed to be such, which has baffled all research as to its origin, "Robert Hood in Barnsdale stood." Editors of our ballad literature have tried to find the original source of this verse. The earliest occurrence of it which they have been able to discover is in Nicholas Udall's translation of the *Apothegms of Erasmus*, first printed in 1542[1]. But the Year Books tell us that it was quoted in Court a hundred and fifteen years earlier than this, and quoted in circumstances which seem to show that even then it was a well-known and familiar phrase[2].

But I must pass on, as there is another matter I want just to touch upon—the vocabulary of the men who wrote these old reports.

As regards vocabulary (Maitland wrote)[3], there is a striking contrast between the earliest and the latest Year Books....A single case of Henry VIII's day shows us "deer, hound, otters, foxes, fowl, tame, thrush, keeper, hunting." We see that already the reporter was short of French words which would denote common objects of the country and gentlemanly sport....But in Edward II's day the educated Englishman was far more likely to introduce French words into his English than English words into his French. The English lawyer's vocabulary was pure and sufficiently copious....Of our reporters we may be far more certain that they could rapidly write French of a sort than that they had ever written an English sentence.

Well, I am not very sure about it, whether those men who wrote "hounds" and so on so wrote because they did not know the French words, or only, being Englishmen, now and again wrote

---

[1] Evans's *Old Ballads* (1810), II, p. 194.

[2] "Annuite porte par un Abbe vers un Parson. Et connta qe labbe et ses predecessors avoyent este seisis de x. s. de rent del Eglise de B. a prendre par les mains le person de temps dont il ny ad memory. *Paston*. Le Dean de Pauls come en droit de sa Eglise de Pauls ad este seisi de xl. s. issant de meme leglise et vous avez este seisis de x. s. parcel de meme cele xl. s. de temps etc. Sans ceo qe vous avez este seisis de x. s. en le maner come vous auez suppose par vostre bref etc. Prest etc. *Rolf*. Robin Hode en Barnesdale stode. Sans ceo qe vous avez este seisis etc. car vostre ple est tant a purpos," etc. etc. Year Books, Pasch. 7 Henry VI, p. 37, case 45.

[2] *Year Book Series* (Selden Society), I, p. xxxvii.

English words more or less unconsciously, without quite
realizing what they were doing. The first year of Henry IV is
a good deal earlier than the case of Henry VIII which Maitland
instances. In 1 Henry IV a man was adjudged to be hanged
and then, before he was dead, to be taken down from the
gallows and eviscerated. The contemporary reporter tells us
how, in execution of this judgment, the man was there "pendue
et let downe arere[1]." I cannot but think that he so wrote
unconsciously, as an Englishman thinking in English, and not
because he really did not know the French for what he wrote
in English. But other reports seem to make it quite certain that
the reporters were so doing. In a report of the Easter Term
of 3 Henry IV, the reporter, in reporting a certain hypothesis,
writes, "car perhaps il poit estre qe" so and so[2]. Here he
certainly knew well enough what the French for "perhaps"
was. And what are we to say about this: "serra la huis et locked
le dore[3]?" or of a reporter who writes "beddes," and then a line
or two further on writes "licts"? One might go on indefinitely
with instances of these old reporters dropping into English
when there cannot be the least doubt that they knew well enough
what the French word was; but enough has been said for my
present purpose. One might, too, indeed, go on indefinitely
discussing the Year Books from one point of view and another,
but an end must be made somewhere; and here, I think, this
lecture must end. And with the close of this lecture, the last
one of my course, I lay down my office, not without some touch
of real regret, for I have been proud and happy to hold it. It has
brought me back to Cambridge for a while, and has given me
some part in the work and life of the University. It only remains
for me to thank you for the attention with which you have listened
to me and to hope that I may have been able to say something
which it was worth your while to hear; to wish you all well in
your various branches of study; and—last word of all—to bid
you good-bye and God-speed.

[1] Year Books, Mich. 1 Henry IV, p. 1, case 1.
[2] Easter, 3 Henry IV, p. 14, case 1.
[3] Hil. 22 Edward IV, p. 45, case 9.

APPENDIX A

I append two further extracts from the Master of the Library of Lincoln's Inn's Report in 1800 to the Select Committee upon Public Records.

As to the manner in which the present editions are printed.—It has been remarked as a matter of regret that "Domesday Book, as printed, is a mere fac-simile, constituting a very large folio, full of abbreviations and signs that cannot be understood without a key and much previous information" (Reeve's *Hist. of E. L.* 1, p. 320). The same description in a great measure is applicable to the printed Year Books, and is certainly a subject of still much juster regret as to them, on account of the more frequent occasions which occur for consulting them. Selden's opinion of the impropriety of printing law books in that manner may be seen from the following passage in his Dissertation on Fleta, concerning the edition to which that Dissertation was prefixed: "Neque enim editio omnino mea est, nec sane, si fuisset, vocabula Exemplaris veteris, ad forensis scriptionis formulam—tot decurtata, et veluti *notis levibus pendentia verba*—(ut de veterum formulariorum scriptione dixit Manilius) adeo retinere permisissem." (Cap. 1.)   (p. 383.)

There is yet another great Desideratum in regard to the Year Books, viz. a full and well-digested General Index to the whole. At present such Indexes as there are in the printed Books are so dispersed in the different volumes[1], are of such unequal merit, and, in general, so scanty and imperfect, that they are of very little use; and the Lawyer generally finds it best to neglect them, and to resort to the different Abridgments of the Law, in order to discover what cases and passages in the Year Books may be applicable to the point he has occasion to examine.

(p. 383.)

---

[1] This is unhappily also true of the *Record Series* and the *Selden Society Series* both individually and jointly.

APPENDIX B

Facsimiles of Selected Passages from Year Book MSS., with Transcripts and Translations.

PLATE I

Lincoln's Inn, Year Books of Edward I (A), fo. 21

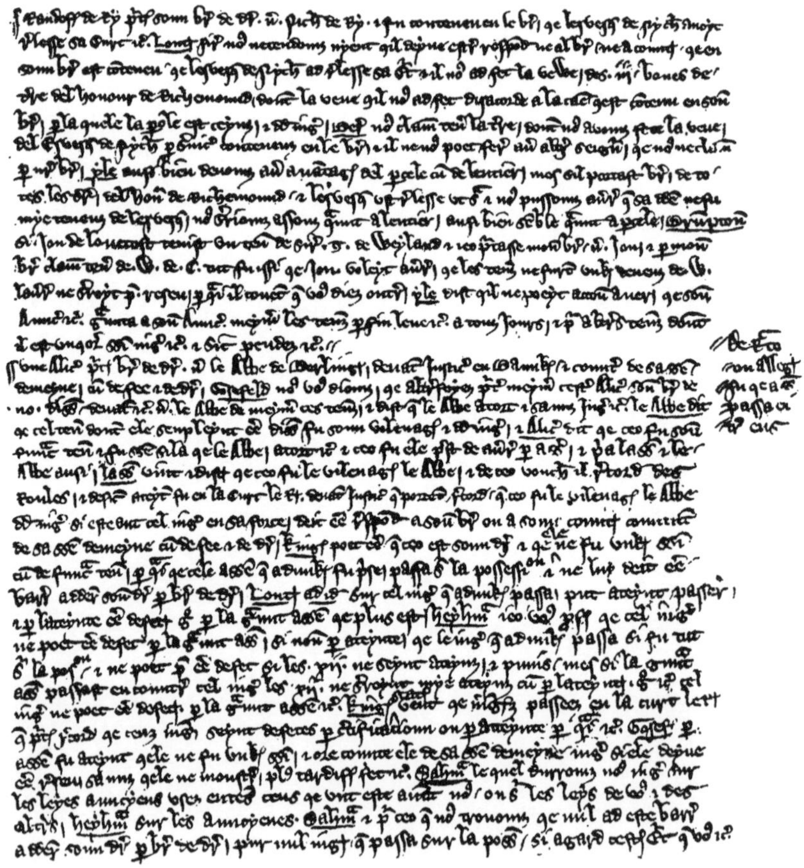

TRANSCRIPT: PLATE I

Randof de Ry porta soun bref de dreit uers Nicholas de Ry et *De Recto.*
fut conteneu en le bref qe lesuesqe de Nychole auoyt / relesse
sa Curt etc.
Louther Sire nous nentendoms nyent qil deyue estre respoundu
ne al bref ne a counte qe en / soun bref est contenu qe lesuesqe
de Nychole ad relesse sa Curt et il nous ad fet la vewe des .iij.
boues de / terre del honour de Richemound dount la vewe qil
nous ad fet disacorde a la case qest contenu en soun / bref par la
quele la parole est ceynz et demandoms iugement. *Bereford* nous
clamons tenir la terre dount nous avoms fete la vue / del Esuesqe
de Nichole par seruices conteneuz en le bref et il ne nous poet
fere auer altre seignur qe nous ne clamons / par nostre bref. *Yerle*
ausi bien deuoms auer auantage del parcele cum de lentier mes
sil portast bref de to/tes les terres del honour de Richemound et
lesuesqe vst relesse vt supra et nous pussoms auerer qe sa demande ne fu / mye tenemenz de lesuesqe nous seriomz assouz
qaunt a lentier ausi bien semble qaunt a parcele. *Brumptone* / si
Ion de louetoft tenist vn tenement de Sire T. de Weyland et ieo
portasse moun bref uers Ion et par moun / bref clamasse tener
de W. de C. tut fu issi qe Ion voleyt auerer qe les tenemenz ne
furent vnkes teneuz de W. / lauerement ne serreyt pas reseu par
quei il couent qe vous diez outre. *Yerle* dist qil ne poyet accioun
auer qe soun / Auncestre etc. graunta a soun Auncestre meyme
les tenemenz par fin leue etc. a touz Iours et pur altres tenemenz
dount / il est vnqore seisi iugement etc. et sic pendet etc.

Vne Alice porta bref de dreit uers le Abbe de Berling deuaunt *De Recto/*
Iustices en Baunk et counta de sa seisine / demeyne cum de fee *ou allege/*
et de dreit. *Gosefeld* nous vous dioms qe altre foyez porta *fu qe*
meyme ceste Alice soun bref de / nouel disseisine deuant etc. *assise/*
uers le Abbe de meyme ces tenemenz et dist qe le Abbe atort *passa*
et saunz Iugement etc. le Abbe dit / qe cel tenement dount ele *en/tre eus.*
senpleynt estre disseisie fu soun vilenage et demaunda iugement
et *Alice* dit qe ceo fu soun / fraunc tenemant et fu seisie si la qe
le Abbe atort etc. et ceo fu ele prest de auerer par assise et pria
lassise et le / Abbe ausi lassise vint et dist qe ceo fu le vilenage
le Abbe et de ceo voucha il recorde des / Roules et desicut
ateynt fu en la Curt le Rei deuaunt Iustices qe portent recorde
qe ceo fu la vilenage le Abbe / demaundoms iugement si esteant
cel iugement en sa force deit estre respoundu a soun bref ou
a soun count countant / de sa seisine demeyne cum de fee et
de dreit. *King* poet estre qe ceo est soun dreit et qe ele ne fu
vnkes seisi / cum de fraunc tenement par quei qe cele assise qe
adunke fu prise passa sur la possessioun et ne luy deit estre /
barre a demander soun dreit par bref de dreit. *Louther ad idem*
sur cel iugement qe adunke passa put ateynt passer / et par
lateynte estre defet ergo par la graunt assise qe plus est. *Heyham*
ieo vous proffre qe cel iugement / ne poet estre defet par la
graunt assise si noun par ateynte qe le iugement qe adunke
passa si fu tut / sur la possessioun et ne poet pas estre defet si
les .xij. ne seynt ateynz et punis mes si la graunt / assise passast
encountre cel iugement les .xij. ne serroynt mye ateynz cum par

lateynt ergo etc. cel / iugement ne poet estre defet par la graunt
assise etc. *King* statut veot qe iugements passeez en la Curt le
Rey / qe porte recorde qe ceuz iugementz seynt defetes par
certificacioun ou par atteynte par quei etc. *Gosefelde* par / assise
fu ateynt qele ne fu vnkes seisi et ore counte ele de sa seisine
demeyne iugement si ele deyue / estre reseu saunz qele ne
moustra plus tardif fet etc. *Saham* le quel durromz nous iugement sur / les leyes auncyenes vsez en tenz ceus qe vnt este
auaunt nous ou sur les leys de vous et des / altres. *Heyham* sur
les auncyenes. *Saham* et pur ceo qe nous trouomz qe nul ad
este barre / a demaunder soun dreit par bref de dreit pur nul iugement qe passa sur la possessioun si agard ceste Curt qe vous etc.

TRANSLATION: PLATE I

[Writ] of
Right.

Randal of Rye brought his writ of right against Nicholas of
Rye and it was stated in the writ that the Bishop of Lincoln had
released [suit at] his Court, etc.

Lowther. Sir, we do not think that [the plaintiff] is entitled
to an answer either to his writ or his count; for in his writ it is
said that the Bishop of Lincoln has released [suit at] his Court;
and he has given us view of three bovates of land within the
Honor of Richmond, and this view which he has given us does
not agree with the case as set out in his writ, by virtue of which
writ the trial is here, and we ask judgment.

Bereford. We claim to hold the land which we have put in
view of the Bishop of Lincoln by the services set out in the writ,
and [the defendant] cannot make us have another lord than the
one we claim to have in our writ.

Herle. We are entitled to advantage ourselves by the parcel
as well as by the whole, and if [the plaintiff] bring a writ of all the
lands of the Honor of Richmond and the Bishop has released
ut supra, and we can aver that what he claims is not part of the
Bishop's tenements, it seems that we shall go quit in respect
of the whole as well as of the part.

Brumpton [J.]. If John of Lovetoft hold a tenement of Sir T.
of Weyland and I bring my writ against John and claim, by my
writ, to hold of W. of C., then, if John wanted to aver that the
tenements were never held of W., the averment would not be
received; and therefore you must say over.

Herle said that the plaintiff could not have any action, for his
ancestor granted to [the defendant's] ancestor these same tenements for ever by a fine levied etc. and in exchange for other
tenements of which he is still seised; judgment etc.; and so the
matter hangs.

Writ of
Right in
which it
was
alleged
that assise
had pass-

One Alice brought a writ of right against the Abbot of Barling
before the Justices in Bank, and she counted of her own seisin
as of fee and right.

Gosefeld. We tell you that this same Alice previously brought
her writ of novel disseisin before etc. against the Abbot in respect
of these same tenements and said that the Abbot wrongfully
and without a judgment etc. The Abbot said that the tenement

of which she complained of being disseised was his villeinage[1] ed be-
and he asked judgment; and Alice said that it was her freehold tween the
and that she was seised of it and that the Abbot wrongfully parties.
etc., and she was ready to aver that by assize; and she prayed
the assize as did the Abbot. The assize came and said that the
tenement was the Abbot's villeinage; and of that he [*sc. Gosefeld*]
vouched the record of the Rolls, and since it was found in the
King's Court before Justices who bear record that this was the
Abbot's villeinage, he asked judgment whether, seeing that that
judgment was still in force, [the plaintiff] was entitled to any
answer to her writ or her count which counted of her seisin as
of fee and right.

King. It may be that this is her right of which she was never
seised as of a freehold and that, consequently, the assize passed
on the possessory right alone, and it ought not to bar her from
claiming her right by a writ of right.

Lowther ad idem. The judgment which was then given can be
attainted and, by such attaint, annulled. It can therefore be
annulled by the great assize, which is of higher authority.

Heyham. I submit to you that that judgment cannot be defeated by the great assize, but only by attaint; for the judgment
that then passed referred wholly to the [right to] possession, and
cannot be annulled unless the twelve [jurors] be attainted and
punished, for if the great assize should pass contrary to that
judgment the twelve would not be [thereby] attainted as they
would be under the [writ of] attaint, therefore etc. that judgment
cannot be defeated by the great assize etc.

King. The statute provides that judgments rendered in a
court of the King which bears record, that such judgments may
be annulled by certificate or by attaint; therefore etc.

Gosefeld. It was found against her by the assize that she was
never seised, and now she counts of her own seisin. [We ask]
judgment if she ought to be received [to such a count] unless she
can show a more recent title etc.

Saham [J.]. Are we to give judgment based on the older laws
observed in the times that were before us or in accordance with
the laws of you and others?

Heyham. On the older laws.

Saham [J.]. Because we do not find that any one has been
barred by any judgment given on the possession from claiming
his [proprietary] right by a writ of right, this Court gives judgment that you etc.

---

[1] *I.e.* held of him by villein services.

PLATE II

Lincoln's Inn, Year Books of Edward I (A), fo. 18

TRANSCRIPT: PLATE II

En bref de forme de doun en le reuertir si dit *Howard* qe vn par my
qy il auoyt counte auoyt relesse et quitecleima et demaunda iugement /
si par luy rien poyet demaunder et mist auaunt fet qe ceo testimoynge.
Kinge il fu dens age le iour de la confeccioun etc. / prest etc. *Howard*
a ceo ne auendrez pas qil vynt iij. annz auaunt la confeccioun de lescrit
deuant les Iustices del / Baunk et fit enrouler ceste Escrit qe cy est et
myst auant vn altre escrit et demaunda iugement desicum deuant la
confeccioun de / nostre escrit fu reseu de Curt cum de plein age si vous
ore deuez estre reseu a dire etc. et qe issint soyt vouchomz recorde / de
roule et prioms qe vous regardez la date de nostre escrit. *Gold.* par la
date ne poez rien estre asserte del age qe / poet estre qe lescrit fu fet .vi.
aunz auant la date qest en lescrit Item par lescrit qe vous mettez auant
ne deuez estre / eyde de nous oster de lauerement etc. qil parle de
altres tenemenz. *Howard* la plus haut choce qe est en Curt si est recorde
dount / encountre ceo qest cy haut ne se deit nul auerement fere mes
nous volomz auerer nostre dit par record iugement si vous deuez /
estre reseu a dire qil apres cele conissaunce fut dens age Item quant
a ceo qe vous dites qe lescrit poet estre eyne de la date / ceo ne poez dire
qe vous auez graunte lescrit bon en tut. iugement si vous poez ex-
cepcioner ore a la forme. *Caue* coment / fu il reseu de plein age. *Howard*
il vint en Curt et conysseit lescrit estre soun fet et le fit enrouler et ne
en/tendomz mye qe les Iustices luy vssent reseu a nule conissaunce
fere sil ne vst este de plein age. *Caue* vn / enfaunt dens age poet venir
en Curt moud bien et porter vn escrit en sa mayn et conustre qe ceo
soyt soun / fet et prier qil seit enroule saunz ceo qil seit chalange de
nule partie et par cele conissance ne serra il pas barre / a demander
vn tenement qil ad aliene apres cel oure et il seit dens age le iour qil
aliene. *Howard* ieo vous moustre qil / ne poet cele conissance fere sil
ne seit de plein age qe pur .ij. choces affermer vent il en Curt sauer pur
soun fet / conustre et affermer et pur fere sa persone acceptable et
de pus qe pur ces .ij. choces vint en Curt et les afferma ne / entendomz
pas qe nule choce qil fit pus cele affirmance puse repeller la et anyntir
cum choce fet dens age etc. / *Caue* la persone nest pas fet acceptable
par cele conissance cum de plein age sil ele ne seit aiugge de pleyn age
par / agarde et pur ceo dites outre. *Howard* de plein age prest etc. et
alii econtra.

William le fiz William fereis porta bref de forme de doun etc. uers

vn Esteuene et demanda vne Carue de terre par la reson qe William de /
Fereys Counte de Derby dona cele terre a William Fereys et a les heirs
de soun cors engendrez et dount il / dist qe la terre a luy deit descendre
cum a fiz et heir par la forme de doun auandit. *Gold.* quei auez de la
forme. *Inge* mist / auant vne chartre qe ceo testimoygne sauer qe la
terre demande fu done en fee tayle ensemblement ou altres terres.
Gold. demanda iugement / desicum la chartre etc. ne testimoygne
mye qe la quantite des tenemenz demandez furent donez etc. *Inge*
tendi lauerement qe meismes / les tenemenz furent contenuz dens la
chartre ensemblement ou altres tenemenz. *Gold.* ne poyet ceo dedire et
dist outre qil ne / poet accioun auer qil dit qe .W. soun pere qy heir
etc. nous dona etc. et obliga luy et ces heirs a la garrante dount / si
nous fuissomz enplede de vn estraunge il nous serroit lye a la garrante
et asseez luy est descendi de part soun pere / et demandoms iugement
si etc. et mist auant la chartre soun pere qe ceo testimoygne. *Inge* par
ceste chartre ne serromz mye / rebote de accioun qar les tenemenz ore
demandez furent alienez pus lestatut et si fin fu leue de meisme les
tenemenz cele / fine ne serroyt mye barre a nous par plus fort ne la
chartre dount nous demandoms iugement desicut vous auez graunte
la forme / et vous ne poez dedire qe lalienacioun fut fet pus statut si
cele chartre nous deit noyre. *Mutford* nous wous dioms / qe .W. de
Fereys counte de Derby dona ces tenemenz longement deuant le
statut par quei nous byoms estre eyde par statut / qe dit *ad dona prius
facta non extenditur. Metingham* si vous entendez *ad dona prius etc.*
al primer doun vous entendez / malement qar eles vnt relacioun al
alienacioun Et pur ceo parlez a vostre clyent et le examynez si soun /
aduersarie eyt rien par descent en fee simplee. *Mutford* il ne poet
accioun auer par la reson auandit et outre vous diomz / qe .W. soun
pere qy heir etc. purchasa vne Carue de terre en Stilbing fereys a vn
.C. et a luy et a ces heirs / simplement et apres sa mort .W. le fiz .W.
qe ore demande entra en meisme la terre cum heir simple dount il / ad
par descente de meysme cely .W. plus qe la terre vaut qest en demande
cum heir simple prest etc. *Inge* tendi lauerement / qil ad nule terre par
descente cum heir simple eynz cum heir especial Ideo Iurata etc.

TRANSLATION: PLATE II

In a writ of formedon in the reverter *Howard* said that he of whose
title [the plaintiff] had counted had released and quitclaimed, and he
asked judgment whether, in virtue of his title, he [the plaintiff] could

claim anything, and he tendered a deed in proof of that [which he had alleged].

King. He was under age on the day of the making [of the deed]; ready [to aver it].

Howard. You will not get to that [averment], for three years before the making of our writing, he came before the Justices of the Bench and had this writing—which is here—enrolled; and he [*Howard*] tendered another writing and asked judgment whether you ought now to be received to say etc., seeing that he was received by the Court as being of full age before the making of our writing; and in proof that this was so we vouch the record of the Roll, and pray that you will look at the date of our writing.

Goldington[1]. You cannot be certified of the age by the date, for it may be that the writing was made six years before the date that is on the writing. Further, by the writing which you tender you cannot be helped in barring us from the averment etc. for it speaks of other tenements.

Howard. The highest authority in Court is the record. No averment, then, that is in contradiction of such high authority ought to be made, and we wish to aver what we have said by the record; [and we ask] judgment whether you ought to be received to say that he was under age after the date of that acknowledgment. Further, as to what you say about the possibility of the writing being older than the date, [we submit that] you cannot say that, for you have admitted that the whole writing is good. Judgment whether you can now take any objection on the form.

Cave [*J.*]. In what way was he received as being of full age?

Howard. He came into Court and acknowledged the writing to be his deed and he had it enrolled, and we submit that the Justices would not have received him to make any acknowledgment unless he had been of full age.

Cave [*J.*]. An infant under age may very possibly come into Court and carry a writing in his hand and acknowledge it as his deed and pray that it be enrolled without being challenged by any one, and he will not be barred by that acknowledgment from claiming a tenement which he has alienated after that time if he were under age on the day on which he alienated it.

Howard. I [will] show you that he could not make that acknowledg-

---

[1] I am not very sure about the expansion of this Serjeant's name.

ment unless he were of full age, for he comes into Court to make two matters plain, namely, to acknowledge and affirm his deed, and to prove that he is personally receivable [by the Court], and since he came into Court for these two purposes and effected them, we do not think that you can reject and avoid anything he did after that affirmation as something that was done while he was under age.

Cave [*J.*]. By such an acknowledgment he does not become personally receivable as one of full age unless he be adjudged by ruling to be of full age; and therefore say over.

Howard. Of full age, ready etc.

And the other side joined issue.

William, the son of William Ferrers, brought a writ of formedon etc. against one Stephen and claimed a carucate of land on the ground that William of Ferrers, Earl of Derby, gave that land to William Ferrers and to the heirs of his body begotten, and touching which he said that the land ought to descend to him, as son and heir, by the aforesaid form of the gift.

Goldington. What have you in proof of the form?

Inge tendered a charter which witnesses this, namely, that the land claimed was given in fee tail together with other lands.

Goldington asked judgment, on the ground that the charter did not show that the amount of the land claimed was the same as that of the tenements given etc.

Inge offered the averment that the same lands [which were claimed] were comprised in the charter, together with other tenements.

Goldington could not deny this, and said over that [the plaintiff] could have no right of action, for he said that W. his father, whose heir he was, gave us etc. and bound himself and his heirs to the warranty, so that if we were sued by a stranger he would be bound to the warranty, and assets have descended to him from his father, and we ask judgment whether etc.; and he tendered the charter of his father which witnesses this.

Inge. We shall not be barred from our action by this charter, for the tenements now claimed were alienated after the statute[1], and if a fine were levied of the same tenements that fine would not bar us, *a fortiori* the charter will not. We therefore ask judgment, seeing that you have admitted the form and cannot deny that the alienation was made after the statute, whether this charter ought to be to our prejudice.

---

[1] *De donis condicionalibus* (Westminster II, c. i).

Mutford. We tell you that W. of Ferrers, Earl of Derby, gave these tenements a long time before the statute, and we are of opinion, therefore, that we ought to be advantaged by the statute which says that it shall not be extended to include grants made previously.

Metingham [*C.J.*]. If you understand the words *ad dona prius* etc. to refer to the first grant you understand them wrongly, for they refer to the alienation. Speak, therefore, to your client and ask him if his opponent has any fee simple by descent.

Mutford. [The plaintiff] cannot have any right of action for the reason before stated, and we tell you further that W. his father, whose heir he is, purchased a carucate of land in Stilbing Ferrers to one C., and to himself and his direct heirs, and after his death W. the son of W., the present plaintiff, entered on the same land as his direct heir, and has thereby by descent from that same W., as his direct heir, land which is worth more than the land now claimed; ready etc.

Inge offered the averment that he has no land by descent as direct heir, but as special heir.

So let a jury etc.

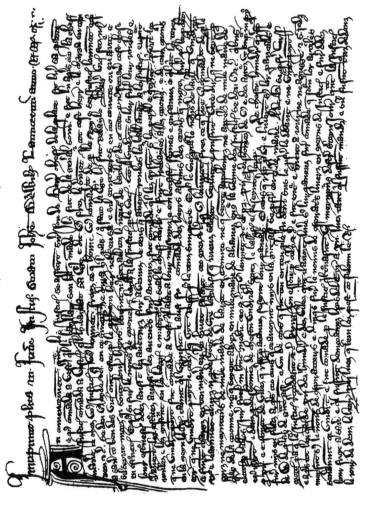

PLATE III

Lincoln's Inn, Hale MS. No. 188, fo. 68

TRANSCRIPT: PLATE III

INCIPIUNT PLACITA IN ITINERE IUSTICIARIORUM CORAM JOHANNE
BEREWIK LAUNCETUN ANNO REGNI REGIS XXX

Au comencement qaunt les Iustices se assisterent sire Ion de Berrewik chef de la place fit lire sa patente / et pus comanda al Vesconte qil
ly baillat son bref qe mande ly fut de la general somouns et fut lu apres
ceo la chef / Iustice comanda a Vesconte qil ly baillat sa verge et dit vous
frez le serment pur tot cest heyr et le charga en ceu / manere ceo oyez
vous Iustices qe vous leument freez ceo qe homme vous comandra de
par le Rey et [les conseils le Rey et]¹ ses Iustices leument [celeret]¹
et pur / ren etc. se deu vous eyde etc. en ce serment ne dirra yl pas
[a mien escient]¹ quo facto le verge ly fut rebayle. Berrewik viconte fetz
nous / a sauer com ben des vicontes ount este pus le procheyn heir ieke
ensa et sil eynt teres en ceo counte ou en autre et / sil seynt morz qi
sount lour heyrs ausint nous fetz auer toz le nouns de baylif de ce
counte et nous fetz auer cest chose / en escrouet. Et pus si furent le
nouns de Coroners baylle a la Iustice par la Veconte et com il vindrent
si lur furent lour roules et / lour escrouestes demaundez ausi cum les
auenturz furent auenuz et ceus qe aueynt roules lez bailleynt auant a
lez Iustices et quant / il aueynt lor escrouez auxsi cum lez auenturs
furent auenuz fut comande qil lez quysent sur lor peryl et² priserent lor /
roulez et lez misterent en lor bagges et misterent le seal le chief clerk et
furent rebayles a lez coronerz Et de ceuz Coroners / qe ne vindrent poynt
fut comande a Vesconte qil alat a lour mesounz et enbotast femmes et
enfaunz et qil prist lor terez / en le meyn le Rey taunt qil venisent et
ausi fu comaunde dez heyrs askuns dez coroners qe mortz furent pus
le procheyn / eyr qe ne vindrent poynt et cely qe vynt respoundi pur
le tenz sun pere Et pus le Vicounte porta le nouns de bayliffs qe vindrent /
et furent chargez en teu manere en lor serment fesaunt ceo oyez etc. qe
vous leument frez ce que homme vous comandra de par le / Rey et
leaument elirrez deus prodeshommes de vostre bayllye qe meuz sachent
veyllent et pussent verite dire qe ne seynt pro/curors ne meyntenours
de nule manere de baret en counte ne qe seyent appelourz ne appelez
[ne meyntenours de appelours ne appelez]³ de nule manere de / play de
la coroune ne qe seyent alyez en nule manere de aliaunz encountre la
venue dez Iustices se deu vous etc. quibus / electis per balliuos Iurati
fuerunt in hunc modum ceo etc. qe vous leaument etc. elirrez xii. prodeshommez de vus et dez autrez vt supra in proximo / Et pus isserent

¹ These words, omitted through the scribe's carelessness, have been
supplied from another MS.
² The miswritten word immediately following is expuncted for erasure.
This underlining with points or dots denoted that the word so underlined
was to be taken as erased.
³ These words are supplied from another MS.

le deuz prodeshommez de chescon vndrid sentz le bayllif et feseynt lor paneal de chescun hundred qe respundent/par xij. et ensement de vilez qe respundent par ataunz feseynt lour paneals et/ceus qe respundent par vj. et liuererent sus lor paneals et furent mys en filaz apres ceo ceus qe ce auoynt mys en la graunt assise se profreynt en tiele manere A. de B. se profre vers I./de W. de play de graunt assise et vn de ceus qe fut tenaunt en teu ple fu demaunde sus le profre le demandant et ne vint poynt. / *Motford* pria qe les Iustices recordasent etc. *Kyng.* vn essone pur cely etc. et fut entre et nient aiourne ne agiugge et sic pendet/Et apres totes les enquestes de xij. dez hundreds et dez uilez quaunt il auoynt liuere sus lur paneuz furent comande qe solum lor articles / meysent sus le nouns de conspiratours Et dunqes furent le nouns de conspiratours liuerez en meyns de Iustices et furent demaundez / seueraument qi vindrent et fut comaunde par le Iustices qil trouasent vi. meynpernours destre serteyn iour quaunt la Iustice/lour freyt a sauer et qil fussent demoraunz hors del Eyr a xij. luez taunt qil fussent mandez et sil fusent trouez dedenz / le iour dedenz le heyr xij. luez qe lem lez prist com feloun le Rey.

TRANSLATION: PLATE III

THE PLEAS BEFORE JOHN BERREWIK, IN THE EYRE OF THE JUSTICES, BEGIN AT LAUNCESTON IN THE THIRTIETH YEAR OF THE KING'S REIGN

At the beginning, when the Justices had taken their seats, Sir John of Berrewik, Chief Justice of the Court, caused his patent to be read, and then he called upon the Sheriff to deliver to him his writ of general summons which had been sent to him, and it was read. After this the Chief Justice ordered the Sheriff to deliver to him his wand, and said, "You shall take the oath for the whole of this Eyre"; and charged him in this fashion: "Hear this, ye Justices, that you shall loyally do what shall be commanded you on the part of the King, and the counsels of the King and of his Justices shall loyally keep secret, and on no account etc., so help you God etc."; and in this oath he shall not say ["to my knowledge"]; which being done the wand was returned to him.

Berrewik. "Sheriff, inform us how many sheriffs there have been since the last Eyre up to the present time, and if they have lands in this county or in any other; and, if any have died, who are their heirs; also let us know all the names of the bailiffs of this county, and let us have this written on a scroll." And then were the names of the coroners delivered to the Justice by the Sheriff; and when they [*i.e.* the coroners] came, their rolls and scrolls were called for from them, and [they were questioned] also as to what misadventures had happened; and those who had their rolls handed them to the Justices, and when they had their scrolls they commanded them at their peril to set out how the misadventures had happened; and they [*i.e.* the Justices] took their rolls and put them in their bags and put thereon the seal of the chief clerk; and they were returned to the coroners. And as to those coroners who did not come, the Sheriff was ordered to go to their houses and to turn out their wives and children and to take their lands into the King's hand until they should come; and in like manner it was ordered touching the heirs of those coroners who had died since the last Eyre and who did not come; and he who came answered for the time of his father. And afterwards the Sheriff brought the names of the bailiffs, who came, and they were charged in this manner in making their oath: "Hear ye this etc. that you shall loyally do what you shall be commanded to do on the King's behalf, and loyally choose two good men of your bailiwick who best may know and will and can tell the truth, and who are not procurers or maintainers of any manner of contention in the county, and who are not appellors or appellees [or maintainers of appellors or appellees] of any kind of pleas of the Crown, and who have not associated themselves in any kind of alliance in view of the coming of the Justices; so help you God etc." These being chosen by the bailiffs were sworn in this wise: "[Hear ye] this etc. that you shall loyally etc. choose twelve good men from among you and the others," as last aforesaid. And then the two good men of each hundred went out without the bailiff and made their panel from each hundred which answered by twelve, and likewise from the vills which answered by the same number they made their panels, and from those which answered by six. And they delivered up their panels, which were put in files. After this, those who had put themselves on the Great Assize proffered themselves in this wise: "A. of B. proffers himself against J. of W. in a plea of the Great Assize"; and one of those who was tenant in such a plea was called on the proffer of the demandant and he did not come. *Mutford* prayed that the Justices would record etc. *Kingesham.* An essoin for him etc. And it was entered and not adjourned nor decision given upon it, and so the plea is pending. And afterwards all the inquests of the twelve of the hundreds and of the vills, when they had given up their panels, were commanded that, in accordance with their articles, they should give up the names of conspirators. And the names of conspirators were then given into the hands of the Justices, and they were called severally, and they came, and it was commanded by the Justices that they should find six mainpernors for their presence on a certain day when the Justices should have them informed of it, and that they should keep themselves twelve miles outside the Eyre until they were sent for; and if, before that day, they were found within twelve miles of the Eyre, they would be arrested as felons to the King.

PLATE IV

British Museum, Addl. MS. 35094, fo. 4

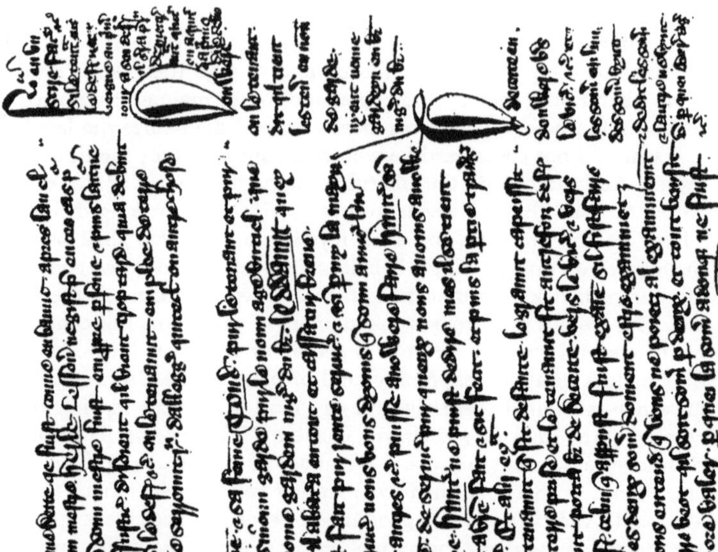

TRANSCRIPT: PLATE IV

Mestre A de B porta soun scire facias vers vn H. dune Dette Nota en
qe fuist conue en baunc apres lan el / iour le defendaunt fit vn / scire
attourne qe voilleit auoir essone soun mestre. *Herle* Lessone facias,
ne gist pas en ceo cas pur / le defendaunt. *Bereford* dit al etc. / si le
attourne qil bosoignereit qe soun mestre fuist en propre persone tenaunt
et puis lattorne / pria allouwaunce de ses aquitances qil auoit ou / le de-
mes les Iustices disoient qil vient trop tard quia debuit / venisse fendaunt
primo die Et ex hoc nota en le scire facias si le defendaunt en ne/ veigne
plee de terre ne / veigne au primer iour il perdrount issint qil ne au primer
serrount resceu dallegger quitecleime ou autre chose / tout /iour a se
veignent il lendemeyn.
defendre /
il serra pas
resceu /
de mettre/
auaunt

Bref de douwere fuist porte vers vn homme et sa femme. quit-
Toudeby pur le tenant et pur / la femme vous dit qil ne clame cleime/ou
rienz en les tenemenz sinoun garde pur le nonnage vn tiel qe / aquitance
tient de luy ceux tenemenz par seruice de chiualre nient nome qe a
gardein iugement du bref. *Le demandaunt* quey / respoundez primo/die
vous al autre. *Hunt* si le bref sabate en partie il abatera en tout breuis.
et cassatur breue.
Douwere/
ou le
tenant/dit

En vne prise des auers Lauowere fuist fait pur rente seruice qil tient/
et seisi par my la mayn / le pleyntif. *Laufer* la ou il auowe pur les tene-
rente seruice nous vous dyoms qe soun auncestre lui / enfeffa menz en
de ceux tenemenz par ceste chartre etc. iugement si pur autres noun / de
etc. puisse auowere faire. *Hunt* seisi / parmy vostre mayn puis garde /
la confeccion de ceste chartre de seruices pur queux nous auoms nyent
auowe / prest etc. *Laufer* est ceo le fait vostre auncestre ou ne nome /
mye. *Hunt* ne puist dedire mes il se tient / a la seisine. *Bereford* gardeyn
faites vostre auowere acordaunt a vostre fait et sic fecit et puis en bref /
la partie trauersa / qe seruices contenuz en la chartre etc. rienz iugement
arreres prest etc. Et alii econtra.
du bref.

Vne femme Porta soun bref de Douwere vers vn tenaunt qe De de-
fit defaute le graunt cape issit / le vicounte retourna qe la partie ceite en /
fuist somouns et la terre prise et le tenaunt fit autrefoiz defaute / douwere
par quei seisine de terre fuist agarde puis le tenaunt porta bref vers / le
de Deceite vers le vicounte et vers / les somonours lun des viconte
somenours vient en court lautre fit defaute celui qe apparust etc. et / les
fuist examine sil fist faire / les somouns et dit qe noun. *Herle* somon-
nous entendoms qe les deux somoneurs deiuent estre examinetz / ours ou
ioyntement et vn nest mie en court par quey nous entendoms lun / des
qe vous ne poietz al examinement / del vn aler saunz lautre. somon-
Bereford depuis qe lei de terre veot qil soit somouns par deux ours vynt
et tout vousit / lautre tesmoigner qil fuit somouns par lui ceo / et dedit
les som-
ouns / et
lautre ne
vynt/ pas

par quei *Bereford* *agarda/* *etc.* ne puist ore valer par quei la somounqe adonqe ne fuist / pas fait solome lei de terre par quei agarde la court qe le tenaunt reeit sa seisine.

TRANSLATION: PLATE IV

Note that in a scire *facias etc. if the tenant or*[1] *the defendant do not come on the first day to defend himself he will not be received to tender a quitclaim or acquittance, but on the first day of the writ only.*

Master A. of B. brought his *scire facias* against one H. of a debt which had been acknowledged in Bank. After the year and the day the defendant appointed an attorney who desired to essoin his master.

Herle. The essoin does not lie in these circumstances for the defendant.

Bereford [C.J.] said to the attorney that it was necessary that his master should appear *propria persona*; and the attorney afterwards prayed allowance of the acquittances which he had, but the Justices said that he came too late, for he ought to have come on the first day. And hence note that in the *scire facias* if the defendant in a plea of land do not come on the first day, he will be a loser to the extent of not being received to allege quitclaim or other matter, even though he come on the next day.

Dower where the tenant said that he held the tenements by way of wardship and was not described as guardian in the writ [and asked] judgment of the writ.

A writ of dower was brought against a man and his wife.

Toudeby for the tenant and for the wife. [The tenant] tells you that he claims nothing in the tenements except wardship during the nonage of one who holds these tenements of him by knight's service, and he is not described as guardian. Judgment of the writ.

The claimant. What answer do you make for the other defendant?

Hunt. If the writ abate in part it will abate wholly.

And the writ is quashed.

In a distraint of cattle the avowry was made for rent service and [the avowant said that he was] seised by the hand of the plaintiff.

Laufer. Whereas he avows for rent service, we tell you that his ancestor enfeoffed him [*sc.* the plaintiff] of these tenements by this charter etc. Judgment whether for other [services than those named therein] he can make avowry.

Hunt. Seised by your hand since the making of this charter of the services for which we have avowed; ready [to aver it].

Laufer. Is this the deed of your ancestor or not?

Hunt could not deny it, but he took his stand on the seisin.

[1] This "or" has the meaning of *aliter* and not of *vel*.

Bereford [*C.J.*]. Make your avowry in accordance with your deed.

And he did so, and then the plaintiff denied that the services set out in the charter etc. were in any respect in arrears. Ready etc. And the other side joined issue.

A woman brought her writ of dower against a tenant who made default. The great *cape* issued. The Sheriff returned that the defendant was summoned and the land taken [into the King's hand], and the tenant previously made default: wherefore seisin of the land was given by judgment. Afterwards the tenant brought a writ of deceit against the Sheriff and against the summoners. One of the summoners came into Court; the other made default. The one who appeared was examined as to whether he served the summons, and he said that he did not.

Herle. We think that the two summoners ought to be examined jointly, and one of them is not in Court; and we think, therefore, that you cannot proceed with the examination of one without the other.

Bereford [*C.J.*]. Seeing that the law of the land is that the defendant should be summoned by two, though the other [*sc.* the absent summoner] should testify that he was summoned by him, that would not now avail aught to prove that the summons was then made in accordance with the law of the land. The Court, therefore, rules that the tenant have his seisin again.

Of deceit in a writ of dower against the Sheriff etc. and the summoners, where one of the summoners came and denied the fact of the summons, and the other did not come; and therefore Bereford ruled etc.

PLATE V

Cambridge University Library, Ff. 3. 12, fo. 24vo

TRANSCRIPT: PLATE V

DE TERMINO SANCTI MICHAELIS ANNO REGNI REGIS EDWARDI
FILII REGIS EDWARDI SECUNDO

Symound de Isepe suit vn appel de la mort William soun friere vers Johan de Ox/tone et lui appela de feloni etc. *Herle* defendit tut maner de feloni assaut engait et quant / etc. la pees etc. sa coroune et sa dignite etc. Et vous dit qe ly ad vn B. ayne de S. / friere William qe mort est de mesme le piere et mesme la miere a qe soun heritage / deueroit descendre a qi naturelement cest accioun est done et cest suit appent etc. iugement si Sy/mownd etc. deyue ore estre receu. *Asseby* il ne veot pas suer ou par cas il est infra sacros / Et S. est de tiel age qil put faire le derein dount aultre est qe sil fut denz age / et nel put pas faire. *Brabazoun* si S. de Isep fust receu a teil appel et il fut par cas sau/ue et puis le ayne friere denz lan et le iour fait soun appel de mesme la mort deuers luy / quele choce ne put estre denaie purceo qe la suit naturalement a luy appent par quel / appel il serra par cas dampne si ensiwereit donqe qe par vne chose il serreit aquite et dampne al appel de ij. appellours qe serreit inconuenient / de ley par quei agarde fut[1] cest court que Iohan de Oxtone en dreit de cest appel ayle quites / et S. purceo qil emprist cest appel qe a ly ne appendit a la prisoun taunqe nous seoms auy/se pur le roi vtrum videlicet debeat apponi modo per regem vel interim moratur etc. quousque / annus et dies transierint et quod constare posset curie quod senior voluerit appellare. Et puis lan / lappelour sura *Rouberie* pur sa deliueraunce et il dit qe il couent qil eit la prisoun et la pe/naunce ouesqes mes ele ne serra pas mout greuose postea le appelour et appelatus fuerunt / manucapti etc. vsque etc.

Appel ou piert qe le puisne friere / auera mye la swte tut / seit le eyne chapelein / et ou dit fut qil swera / apres lan etc.

---

[1] This word is carelessly interpolated here, and does not occur in other MSS.

TRANSLATION: PLATE V

OF THE MICHAELMAS TERM IN THE SIXTH YEAR OF THE REIGN
OF KING EDWARD THE SON OF KING EDWARD

Appeal,
by which
it appears
that the
younger
brother
[of the
dead man]
shall not
have the
suit, even
though
the elder
brother
be in holy
orders.
And it
was said
that he
[i.e. the
appellor]
might sue
for his de-
liverance
after the
year.

Simon of Isep sued an appeal for the death of his brother William against John of Oxton and appealed him of felony, etc.

Herle denied all manner of felony, assault, waylaying and all that is against [the King's] peace, his crown and dignity etc. And [he said] we tell you that there is one B., older than Simon, brother of William the dead man by the same father and the same mother, to whom the heritage ought to descend and to whom this action is naturally given and this suit belongs etc. Judgment whether Simon etc. ought now to be received.

Ashby. [The elder brother] will not sue, or maybe he is in holy orders; and Simon is of such an age that he can make the proof. And so it is otherwise than if he were within age and could not make it.

Brabazoun [C.J.K.B.]. If Simon of Isep were received to make this appeal and the appellee happened to be acquitted, and afterwards, within the year and the day, the elder brother made his appeal against him for the same death, it could not be denied, for the suit naturally belongs to him, and by that appeal it might happen that the appellee would be condemned; and so it might come about that the appellee would be condemned on the appeal of one and acquitted on the appeal of another of two appellors, which would be an incongruity in law. Wherefore this Court rules that John of Oxton go quit in respect of this appeal, and that Simon, because he took upon himself this appeal which does not belong to him, go to prison until we are advised on the King's behalf whether [the appellee] is now to be apposed[1] on the King's behalf, or whether the matter is to be delayed until the year and the day have elapsed and it be known to the Court whether the elder brother will prosecute an appeal.

[1] When an appeal was quashed for formal reasons the appellee was "apposed" by the Court, *i.e.* he was put to answer the accusation, on the King's prosecution, as if he were indicted.

And after the year the appellor sued *Ronbury* [*J.*] for his deliverance. And [*Ronbury*] said that he must have prison and penance[1] too, but that it will not be very grievous.

Afterwards the appellor and the appellee were mainprised etc., until etc.

---

[1] On the nature of this punishment information is wanting.

PLATE VI

Lincoln's Inn, Hale MS. 139, fo. 132vo

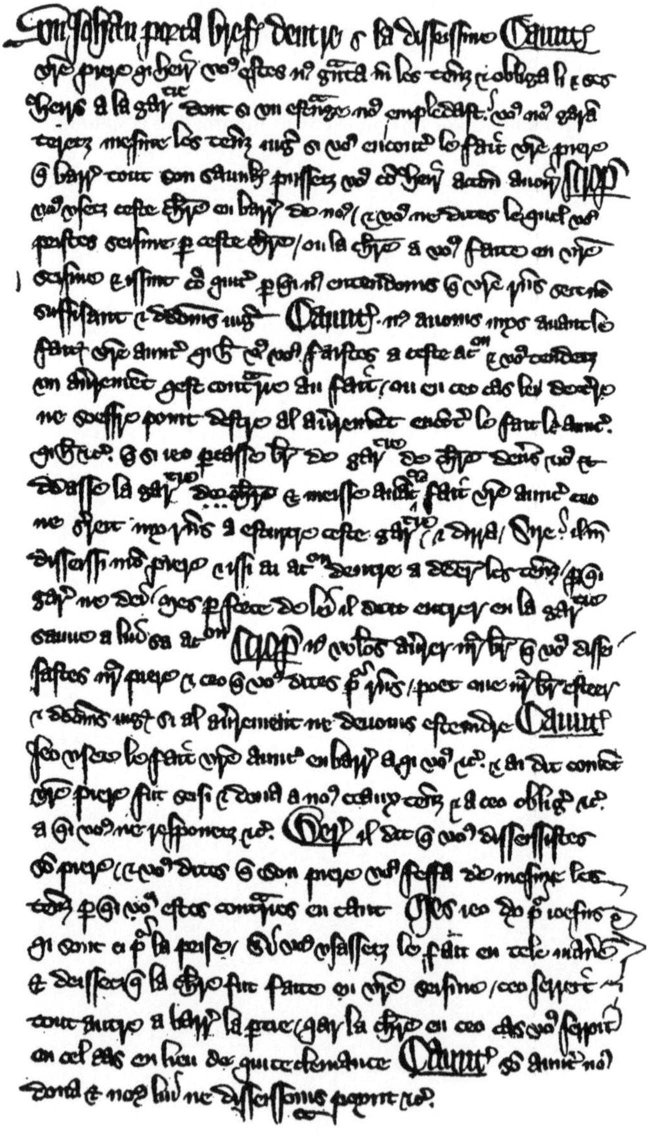

TRANSCRIPT: PLATE VI

Vn Iohan porta bref dentre sur la disseisine. *Cauntebridge* / vostre piere qi heir vous estes nous graunta mesme les tene-ments et obliga li et ses / heirs a la garauntie dont si vn estraunge nous empledast vous nous garaun/teretz mesme les tenemenz iugement si vous encontre le fait vostre piere / qe barre tout son saunk pussetz vous com heir accioun auoir. *Scrope* / vous vsetz ceste chartre en barre de nous et vous ne dites le quel vous / pristes seisine par ceste chartre ou la chartre a vous faite en vostre / seisine et issint com quiteclemance par quei nous entendoms qe vostre respouns seit non / suffisant et demandoms iugement. *Cauntebridge* nous auoms mys auant le / fait vostre auncestre qi heir vous vous faistes a ceste accioun et vous tendetz / vn auerement qest contrarie au fait ou en ceo cas lei de terre / ne soeffre point destre al auerement encountre le fait le auncestre / qi heir etc. qe si ieo percasse bref de garauntie de chartre deuers vous et / demandasse la garauntie de chartre et meisse auant le fait vostre auncestre ceo / ne serreit my respouns a esturtre ceste garauntie et dirra Sire il mesme / disseisi mon piere et issi ai accioun dentre a demander les tenemenz par qei / garauntie ne dei mes par force de lei il deit entrer en la garauntie / sauue a lui sa accioun. *Scrope* nous voloms auerer nostre bref qe vous dis-sei/sastes nostre piere et ceo qe vous dites pur respouns poet oue nostre bref esteer / et demandoms iugement si al auerement ne deuoms esteindre. *Cauntebridge* / Ieo vsee le fait vostre auncestre en barre a qi vous etc. et ai dit coment / vostre piere fut seisi et dona a nous ceaux tenemenz et a ceo obliga etc. / a qei vous ne responetz etc. *Bereford* il dit qe vous disseisistes / son piere et vous dites qe son piere vous feffa de mesme les / tenemenz par qei vous estes contraries en tant Mes ieo dy pur ioesnes / qi sont ci pur le prise si vous vsassetz le fait·en tele manere / et deissetz qe la chartre fut faite en vostre seisine ceo serreit / tout autre a barrer la partie qar la chartre en ceo cas vous serreit / en cel cas en lieu de quiteclemance. *Cauntebridge* son auncestre nous / dona et nous lui ne disseissoms poynt etc.

TRANSLATION: PLATE VI

*Entry on
novel dis-
seisin.*   One John brought a writ of entry on novel disseisin.

Cambridge. Your father, whose heir you are, granted us these same tenements and bound himself and his heirs to the warranty. If, then, a stranger sued us you would warrant these same tenements to us. [We ask] judgment whether you can have any right of action as his heir in face of your father's deed, which bars all descended from him.

Scrope. You are using this charter to bar us, and you do not say whether you got seisin by virtue of this charter, or whether the charter was made for you during your seisin, and so was in the nature of a quitclaim. We, therefore, do not think that your answer is sufficient, and we ask judgment [on this point].

Cambridge. We have tendered the deed of your ancestor, whose heir you make yourself to be, [in bar of] this action, and you offer an averment which is in contrariety with the deed, where, in such circumstances, the law of the land does not allow you to get to an averment against the deed of your ancestor, whose heir etc.; for if I were to purchase a writ of warranty of charter against you and claim warranty of the charter and tender the deed of your ancestor, it would be no answer, sufficient to avoid the warranty, if he [*i.e.* the plaintiff] says: "Sir, he himself disseised my father and so I have an action of entry[1] to claim the tenements, and so I am not bound to the warranty"; but by force of law he must enter into the warranty, his right of action being reserved to him.

Scrope. We wish to aver our writ, that you disseised our father; and what you say by way of answer can be quite compatible with our writ; and we ask judgment whether we ought not to get to the averment.

Cambridge. I am using your ancestor's deed in bar, to which you etc., and I have said how your father was seised and granted these tenements to us and bound himself to that etc.; to which you make no answer etc.

Bereford [C.J.]. He says that you disseised his father, and you

---

[1] *I.e.* by a writ of entry *sur disseisine*.

say that his father enfeoffed you of these same tenements; and as to that much you are in direct contradiction; but I say, for the [instruction of the] young men who are here for the purpose of learning, that if you use the deed in such a way and say that the charter was made during your seisin, it would, in such case, have effect as a quitclaim.

Cambridge. His ancestor granted to us, and we did not disseise him etc.

PLATE VII

British Museum, Addl. MS. 35116, fo. 145

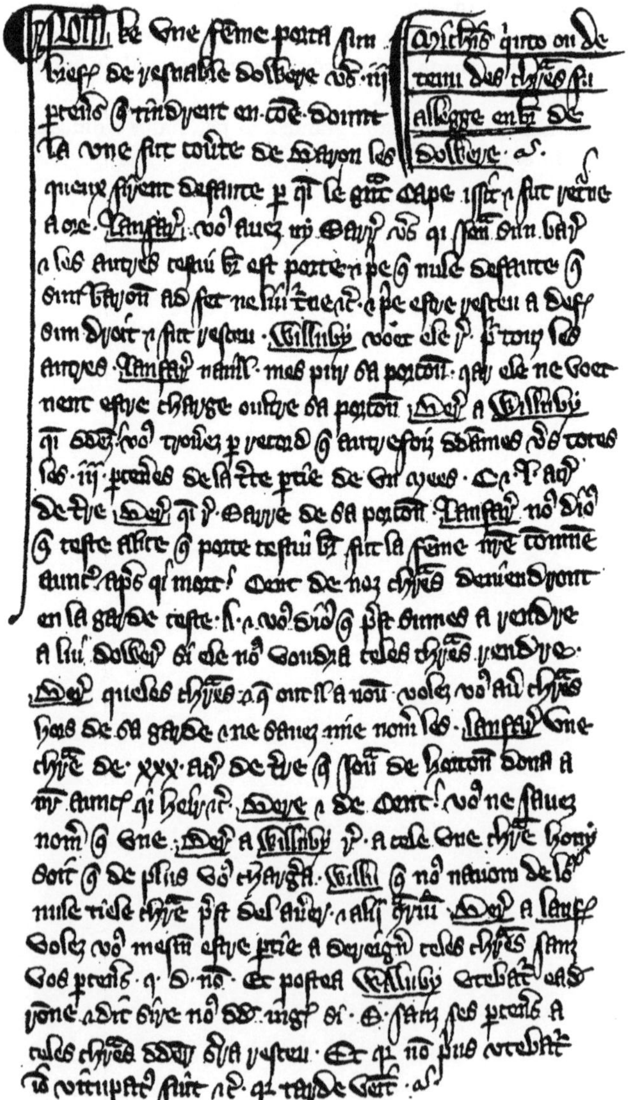

TRANSCRIPT: PLATE VII

Nota ke vne femme porta sun / bref de resnable dowere vers iiij /
parceners qe tindrent en commune dount / la vne ⎧Michaelis quinto
fut couerte de Baron les / queux firent defaute par ⎪ou detenu des
qei le graunt Cape issit et fut returne / a ore. *Lau-* ⎨chartres fu allege
fare vous auez icy Sarre vers qi Iohan sun baron / et ⎩en bref de douere
les autres cestui bref est porte et prie qe nule defaute qe / sun baroun
ad fet ne lui turne etc. et prie estre resceu a defendre / sun droit et fut
resceu. *Willuby* voet ele respoundre pur touz les / autres. *Laufare*
nanil. mes pur sa purcion qar ele ne voet / nent estre charge oultre
sa porcion. *Bereford* a *Willuby* / qei demandez vous trouerez par record
qe autrefoiz demandames vers totes / les .iij. parceners de la terce
partie de vn mees .C. et .I. acres / de terre. *Bereford* qei respounde
Sarre de sa porcion. *Laufare* nous dioms / qe ceste alice qe porte cestui
bref fut la femme nostre commune / auncestre apres qi mort Cent
de noz chartres deuiendront / en la garde ceste A. et vous dioms qe
prest sumes a rendre / a lui dowere si ele nous voudra celes chartres
rendre. / *Bereford* queles chartres et qe ont il a noun volez vous auer
chartres / hors de sa garde et ne sauez mie nomer les. *Laufare* vne /
chartre de .xxx. acres de terre qe Iohan de Hortone dona a / nostre
auncestre qi heir etc. *Bereford* et de cent vous ne sauez / nomer qe vne.
Bereford a *Willuby* respoundez a cele vne chartre hony / soit qe de plus
vous chargera. *Willuby* qe nous nauom de lour / nule tiele chartre prest
del auerer et alii contrarium. *Bereford* a *Laufare* / volez vous mesme
estre partie a dereigner celes chartres sanz / vos parceners quasi diceret
non. Et postea *Willuby* vtebatur eadem / racione et dit Sire nous demandoms iugement si .S. sanz ses parceners a / celes chartres demander
serra resceu. Et quia non prius vtebatur / ideo vituperatus fuit etc.
quia tarde venit.

TRANSLATION: PLATE VII

Note that a woman brought her writ of reasonable dower against four parceners who held in common, one of whom was *coverte* with a husband. They made default and thereupon the great *cape* issued and return was now made.

{Of the Michaelmas [term] of the fifth [year], where detinue of charters was alleged in a writ of dower

Laufer. You have here Sarah, against whom and John, her husband, and the others this writ is brought, and she prays that no default which her husband has made may be used to her disadvantage, and she prays to be received to defend her right—and she was received.

Willoughby. Does she wish to answer on behalf of all the others?

Laufer. No, but for her own portion [only], for she does not wish to be answerable beyond her own portion.

Bereford [C.J.] to Willoughby. What are you claiming?

[*Willoughby.*] You will find by the record that we previously claimed against the three[1] parceners of the third part of a messuage [and] a hundred and one acres of land.

Bereford [C.J.]. What does Sarah answer as to her portion?

Laufer. We say that this Alice who brings this writ was the wife of our common ancestor, after whose death a hundred of our charters came into the custody of this Alice, and we tell you that we are ready to render her dower if she will surrender these charters.

Bereford [C.J.]. What charters are they and how are they named? Do you want to get charters out of her custody which you cannot name?

Laufer. One of them is a charter in respect of a hundred acres of land which John of Horton gave to our ancestor, whose heir [we are].

Bereford [C.J.]. And of a hundred charters you can name only one?

Bereford [C.J.] to Willoughby. Answer as to this one charter. It would be shameful that he should charge you with more.

Willoughby. [We say] that we have no such charter of theirs; ready to aver it.

And the other side joined issue on this.

---

[1] On Sarah's subsequent marriage a new writ must have been issued including her husband amongst the defendants.

Bereford [*C.J.*] to *Laufer*. Do you alone, without your parceners, wish to be party to prove your right to the possession of these charters? —implying that she could not.

And *Willoughby* afterwards used the same argument and said: Sir, we ask judgment whether Sarah will be received to claim these charters without her parceners.

And because he had not availed himself of this point previously he was blamed, because he was so slow to make use of it.

PLATE VIII

Cambridge University Library, Gg. 5. 20, fo. 60vo

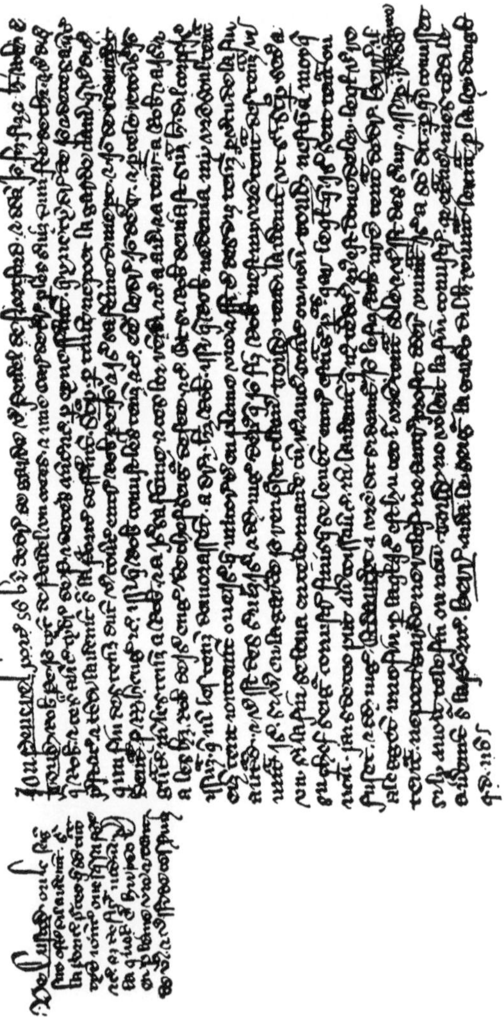

TRANSCRIPT: PLATE VIII

DE TERMINO PASCHE. ANNO SEXTO

Ion Peuerel porta son bref de dreit de garde vers Peuerel de *De Cus-*
Nortford et demanda Ion fiz fiz et heir Robert etc. / *Toudeby* *todia ou*
le seignur
Robert Pere Ion tynt de Peuerel vn mees et vne Carue de terre / *fut oste*
par les seruices dun fee de chiualer et vous dioms / qe Robert et *dil auere-*
ment sur /
ces auncestres tyndrent de P. et de ces auncestres etc. par eyne *la priorite*
feffement qey ne tyndrent de Ion et de ces auncestres / prest etc. *pur ceo*
qe son
et tendi lauerement sur la priorite de feffement. *Scrope* par taunt *tenaunt /*
ne poet la garde clamer qe vous dioms / qun fin des tenemenz *tynt*
iointe-
dunt vous countez entre Robert Pere Ion et Isabelle sa femme *ment*
dune part et Ion de C. dautre part / deuant Sire R. Hengham etc. *ouesqe*
sa femme/
issi qe Robert conust les tenemenz etc. estre le dreit Ion de C. et *etc.*
pur cele reconusance Ion / graunta mesme les tenemenz a Robert
et a Isabelle sa femme et ces lor rendi etc. a auer et a tenir a
Robert et a Isabelle et / a les heirz Robert 'de Isabelle engendrez
de chef seignur de fee etc. Et si Robert deuiast saunz heir dil
corps Isabelle / issuanz qe mesme les tenemenz demorassent a
dreiz heirz Robert issi qe Robert ne deuia my vostre soul tenaunt / einz tent iointement oue Isabelle qe uncore est en pleine
vie et seisi est des diz tenemenz par vertu de la fin / auant dit et
vous seisi des seruicez Isabelle et demandoms iugement depuis
qe Ion fitz Robert nest mye vostre tenaunt des tenemenz vi/-
uaunt Isabelle si vous en la garde Ion ren pusset clamer. *Toudeby*
tendi lauerement vt supra. *Scrope* seoms a / vn si la fin se leua
en cele manere cum nous auoms counte ou noun. *Toudeby* nest
pas a moy qe / su chef seignur conustre finis qe se leuent entre
estraunge purchasours qar lequel Isabelle seit tenaunt ou / noun
pais de ceo put auer conissaunce mesme lauerement qe nous
tendoms nous est done de ley lequel vous re/fuset et demandoms iugement. *Et dautre part* a vostre dit si demurt Ion le fiz
Robert nostre tenaunt de dreit. *Bereford* il / aleggent une fin
par laquelle Isabelle est hu ceo ior vostre tenaunt sole et vous
seisi des seruicez issi par resoun de defaute de / tenaunt ne poet
garde ne relef ne autre profit demander viuaunt Isabelle a son dit
par qei conusset / si ly auoit tele fin ou noun. *Toudeby* non
voleit la fin conustre quia [inter] extraneos mes tendi le / auerement sur la priorite. *Bereford* auera le seignur la garde dil heir
viuaunt le tenaunt par la ley dengleterre / quasi diceret non.

TRANSLATION: PLATE VIII

[PLEAS] OF THE EASTER TERM IN THE SIXTH
YEAR [OF EDWARD II]

Of Ward-
ship;
where the
lord was
barred
from an
averment
of priority
[of feoff-
ment]
because
his tenant
held
jointly
with his
wife etc.

John Peverel brought his writ of right of wardship against Peverel of Northford and claimed John, son and heir of Robert etc.

Toudeby. Robert, John's father, held a messuage and a carucate of land of Peverel by the services [due] from one knight's fee, and we tell you that Robert and his ancestors held of P. and his ancestors etc. by an older feoffment than that by which they held of John and his ancestors; ready [to aver it] etc. and he offered the averment on the priority of feoffment.

Scrope. He cannot claim the wardship for such a reason, for we tell you that a fine of the tenements named in your count [was levied] between Robert, John's father, and Isabel his wife, of the one part, and John of C. on the other part, before Sir R. Hengham etc., by which Robert recognised the tenements etc. as being the right of John of C., and in consideration of this recognition John granted the same tenements to Robert and Isabel, his wife, and surrendered them to them etc. to have and to hold to Robert and Isabel and to the heirs of Robert of Isabel begotten, of the chief lord of the fee etc. And if Robert should die without heir of the body of Isabel issuing, then the same tenements were to remain to the right heirs of Robert. Consequently, Robert did not die your sole tenant, but he held jointly with Isabel, who is still in full life and is seised of the said tenements by virtue of the aforesaid fine, and you are seised of Isabel's services; and, seeing that John, son of Robert, is not your tenant of the tenements so long as Isabel is alive, we ask judgment whether you can claim aught in the wardship of John.

Toudeby offered the averment as above.

Scrope. Let us be at one on the point whether a fine was levied after the manner we have counted or not.

Toudeby. It is not for me, who am chief lord[1], to admit fines levied between strange purchasers[2], for the question whether or not Isabel is tenant is one which lies within the competence of the country[3] [to determine]; and that same averment which

---

[1] *I.e.* the chief lord's counsel.
[2] *I.e.* between whom and me there is no privity.
[3] *I.e.* of a jury of the venue.

we offer is given to us by the law, and you refuse it; and we ask judgment. And further, according to what you say, John, the son of Robert, remains our tenant of right.

Bereford [*C.J.*]. They allege a fine by which Isabel is to-day your sole tenant and you are seised of her services, and so, according to what they say, you cannot, so long as Isabel is alive, claim wardship or relief or any other profit; and therefore say whether there be such a fine or not.

Toudeby would not admit the fine because it was levied between strangers [to him], but he offered the averment on the priority [of feoffment].

Bereford [*C.J.*]. Would the lord have the wardship of the heir during the life-time of the tenant by the law of England[1]? —implying that he would not.

---

[1] *I.e.* the tenant by the curtesy.

APPENDIX B

PLATE IX

Cambridge University Library, Dd. 9. 64, fo. 74

TRANSCRIPT: PLATE IX

DE TERMINO SANCTI MICHAELIS ANNO REGNI REGIS EDWARDI FILII REGIS EDWARDI SEPTIMO. BEREFORD

Thomas Badel porta son cessauit vers William Mustel et Iohan Cessauit. Mustel qi tiendrent de li par homage / et feaute et par escuage et par certein seruice etc. des quex seruices il fut par my lour main etc. *Scrope* nous vous dioms qe / Richard vostre Ael qi heir vous estes en la seysine I. larcher tenaunt de mesme les tenemenz par cel fet relessa et quiteclama tut son / dreit etc. Sauue a li et a ses heirs vne liuere de comyn par an pur touz seruices le quel Iohan nous enfeffa de mesme les / tenemenz pus estatut par son fet qe cy est issint vous dioms nous qe nous tenoms de vous par les seruices auanditz compris / deinz cel fait les quex seruices nous sumes prist a faire et demandoms iugement si encountre le fait vostre ael qi heir vous estes peussez / rien demander. *Miggele* a cel fait nauoms mestre a respoundre qe nous portoms cesti bref a recouerir le demene par le cesser des seruices / des quex seruices nous sumes seruy par my vostre mayn et si vous feussez receu adefere les seruices des quex vous auetz / cesse ce serreit adefere les seruices des quex nous auoms este seisi les quex vous ne dedites pas ne vous ne deditez / pas le cesser le quel nous auoms auere iugement. *Scrope* a ce plee poet homme prendre diuerse issue come a respoundre as seruices / ou a respoundre al demene et deloure qe nous sumes prest afaire les seruices qe vostre auncestre qi heir etc. reserua par son fait etc. iugement. / *Herle* cesti bref est done en lieu de destreynt et par launciene ley si ie feusse par voye dauowerie vous nauerez qe .ij. / respouns ou a desclamer ou a dire nient seysi et depuys qe vous auez conu qe vous estes estraunge purchasour et / nous voloms auerer qe nous fumes seisi par my vostre main iugement etc. Estre ceo si la curt me chase a respoundre a cel / fet ie plederai auxi haut en ce bref qest done par statut a recouerir le demene cum en vn ne vexes qe ne / gist nient pur purchacour. *Scrope* nous auoms veu estrange purchacour sei descharge en le plee de prise / des auers par mye especialte auxi come priue. *Bereford* si vous ne poez par cel fait benefiz auer vous ne deuez / iammes estre descharge par nule manere de ley et a doner a ly recouerir par le cessauit des seruices qe sount esteinz / en sa persone par le fait son auncestre qi heir etc. duresse serreit.

TRANSLATION: PLATE IX

[PLEAS] OF THE TERM OF ST MICHAEL IN THE SEVENTH
YEAR OF THE REIGN OF KING EDWARD SON OF
KING EDWARD. BEREFORD[1]

Cessauit.　　Thomas Badel brought his *cessauit* against William Mustel
and John Mustel who held of him by homage and fealty and by
escuage and by service certain etc.; of which services he was
[seised] by their hands, etc.

Scrope. We tell you that Richard your grandfather, whose
heir you are, during the seisin of J. the Archer, tenant of these
same tenements, by this deed released and quitclaimed all his
right etc., reserving to himself and his heirs a pound of cumin
every year in lieu of all services; and the same John enfeoffed us
of the same tenements after the [passing of the] statute[2] by his
deed, which is here; so we tell you that we hold of you by the
services aforesaid set out in this deed, which services we are
ready to render; and we ask judgment whether you can claim
anything against the deed of your grandfather, whose heir you
are.

Miggeley. To this deed we are under no obligation to answer,
for we are bringing this writ to recover the demesne by reason
of your ceasing to render the services, of which services we are
seised by your hand; and, if you were received to annul the
services which you have ceased to render, that would be to annul
the services of which we have been seised, [services] which you
do not deny, nor do you deny the cessation [in the render of
them] which we have averred. Judgment.

Scrope. In this plea one may take different issues, either
making answer in respect of the services or answering in respect
of the demesne; and since we are ready to render the services
which your ancestor, whose heir etc., reserved by his deed etc.,
[we ask] judgment.

Herle. This writ is given in lieu of distraint; and, by the older
law, if I were proceeding by way of avowry, you would have only
two answers [open to you], either to disclaim [the tenancy] or

[1] Denoting that it was Bereford C.J.'s copy. Possibly each of the
Justices was furnished with his own copy; and there was also the
King's copy marked "Rex."

[2] The statute *Quia emptores.*

to say that we were not seised [of the services]; and since you have admitted that you are a strange purchaser and we wish to aver that we were seised by your hand, judgment etc. Again, if the Court forces me to answer that deed, I can plead as high [*i.e.* of matters as far back] in this writ, which is given by statute for the recovery of the demesne, as in a *ne vexes*, which a purchaser cannot use[1].

Scrope. We have seen a strange purchaser, equally with one who was privy, discharge himself by virtue of a specialty in a plea of distraint of cattle.

Bereford [*C.J.*]. If you cannot be helped by this deed you will never be entitled to be discharged by any other way of law; and to give the plaintiff, by the *cessauit*, recovery of services which are extinguished in him by the deed of his ancestor, whose heir etc., would be a hardship [on the defendant].

---

[1] The *ne vexes* was not open to a purchaser. It was always ancestral and could be used only when the tenant and his ancestors had held of the lord and his ancestors.

APPENDIX B

PLATE X
Lincoln's Inn, MS. 189, fo. 61

TRANSCRIPT: PLATE X

Vn home et sa feme porterent bref de douere deuers Brayan de Cornewayne et vn autre / de la tierce partie de la moyte del manere de H. de dowment le premer baroun la feme. / *Huls* nous demaundoms la view. *Hill* nostre baroun murust seisi et demaundoms iugement si le vewe deuez auer / etc. *Huls* le baroun ne murust seisi de fe symple ne de fe taille par qy iugement et prioms / la vewe etc. *Hill* et nous demaundoms iugement del houre qe nous auoms dit qe nostre baroun / murust seisi quel chose nous voilloms auerer et le quel vous ne deditez mie et de / quel estate qil murust seisi vous estez ouste de la vewe par qy iugement etc. *Huls* / si le baroun ne murust seisi de fee symple ne de fe taille donqes le baroun ne murust / pas seisi de tiel estate qe la femme fuist dowable par qy il est resoun donqes qe nous / eioms le vewe et puis *Huls* wayua le vewe et disclayma par attorne pur / lautre noun etc. et puis Brayan par *Huls* dist accioun ne deuez auer qar nous vous / dioms qe la feme demaundant al tens del murant de soun baroun fut la neef mesme cestuy B. / regardaunt a soun manere de B. et il fuist seisi de luy si comme de soun naif et dioms / qe soun baroun murust saunz issue apres qi mort Brean entra en mesme le manere comme frere / et heire et issint le manere en soun possessioun dount ele demaunde etc. a quell tens ele fuist soun / neife par qy chescun manere de droit de dowere en soun possessioun fut estent et demaundoms iugement si / accioun etc. *Hill* nous vous dioms par voie de protestacioun qe la femme est fraunc et de fraunc / estate etc. et dioms qe le baroun de qy dowement etc. fuist seisi de mesme le manere et murust seisi / de mesme le manere etc. apres qy mort entra vn R. comme fitz et heir et soun estate continua / tanqe la feme et soun baroun a ore entremarie-rent auaunt quell tens vous nauiez riens / en le fraunc tenement quell chose nous voilloms auerer si etc. et issint fraunc deuers vous / et dreit dauer dowere et coment qe le fraunctenement auient a vous celle nulle ley moy mette / a respoundre par qy iugement et prioms seisin de terre etc. *Huls* et nous demaundoms iugement del houre qe vous ne deditz / pas qe vous fuistez nostre naife al tens de murant del baroun regardaunt etc. ne qe nous fussoms seisi / de vous et vnquore estez nostre naif en dreit en quell cas qaunt le manere est en / nostre possessioun chescun dreit de dowere fuist esteint le quell manere est vnquore en nostre / possessioun par qy nous demaundoms iugement si accioun deuers nous deuez auer etc. mes nos a demurer etc.

TRANSLATION: PLATE X

A man and his wife brought a writ of dower against Brayan of Corn-wayne and another [defendant] for the third part of the moiety of the manor of H. as the wife's dower from her first husband.

Huls. We claim the view.

Hill. Our husband died seised, and we ask judgment whether you are entitled to have view etc.

Huls. The husband did not die seised of a fee simple nor of a fee tail, and we therefore ask judgment and pray the view etc.

Hill. And we ask judgment since we have said that our [first] husband died seised, a matter which we are ready to aver and you do not deny; and since he had an estate of seisin when he died you are barred from the view; therefore judgment etc.

Huls. Unless the husband died seised of a fee simple or a fee tail, the husband did not therefore die seised of such an estate that the wife was dowable, and therefore it is right that we should have the view.

And afterwards *Huls* waived the view and, by the attorney, disclaimed [tenancy] on behalf of the other named [defendant]; and afterwards Brayan said by *Huls*: You are not entitled to have an action, for we tell you that the woman who claims was, at the time of her husband's death, the naif of this same Brayan, regardant to his manor of B., and he was seised of her as his naif; and we tell you that her husband died without issue, and after his death Brayan entered on the same manor as brother and heir, and in this way the manor of which she claims etc. is in his possession; and at that time she was his naif, and, consequently, all manner of right of dower which she had was extinguished; and we ask judgment whether she has any right of action etc.

Hill. We tell you, by way of protestation, that the woman is a free woman and of free estate etc.; and we say that the husband, of whose endowment etc., was seised of this same manor and died seised of the same manor etc., and, after his death, one R. entered as son and heir, and continued his estate until the woman and her present husband intermarried, before which time you had nothing in the freehold; and this we will aver if you [want to deny it], and so the woman is free in respect of you and [has a] right to have dower; and though the freehold came to you, I am obliged by no law to make any answer as to that fact, and so [we ask] judgment and pray seisin of the land etc.

Huls. And we ask judgment, seeing that you do not deny that you were our naif regardant etc. at the time of the death of your husband, nor that we were seised of you, and you still are our naif in right; in which circumstances all right to dower was extinguished while the manor is in our possession, and that manor is still in our possession; and we therefore ask judgment whether you ought to have any action against us; but he did not dare to demur on that point.

PLATE XI

Lincoln's Inn, Hale MS. 137 (2), fo. 86

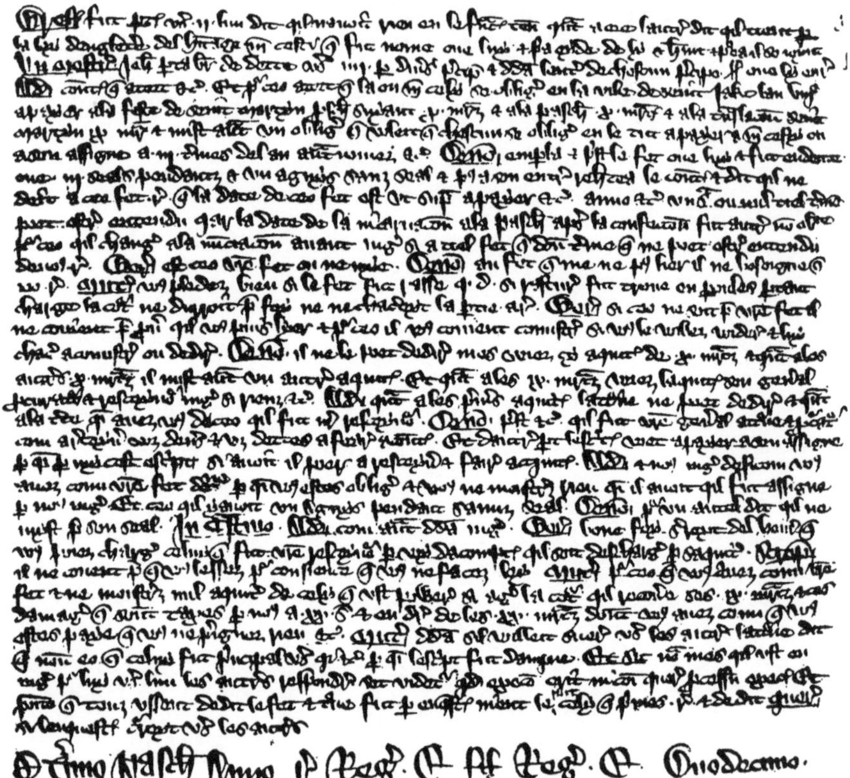

TRANSCRIPT: PLATE XI

Bref fut porte vers .ij. lun dit qil nauoit rien en le fraunc tenement
quant a ore lautre dit qil tient par / la lei dengleterre del heritage mesme
cesti qe fut nome oue luy et pria eyde de ly et habuit et postea il se
ioynt / oue ly en respouns.

Vn Mestre Iohan porta bref de dette vers iiij. par diuerse precipes
et demanda lentier de chescun precipe. / *Aldborough* counta qe atort etc.
Et pur ceo atort qe la ou mesme cely se obliga en la vile de Seint Jake
lan viij. / a payer a la feste de Seint Martyn proschein suyant .x. marz
et ala pasche .x. marz et ala translacioun Seint / Martyn .ix. marz et
mist auant vn obligacion qe voleit qe chescun se obliga en le tut a payer
a mesme cesty ou / a son assigne a .iij. termes del an auant nomez etc.
Denom emparla et prist le fet oue luy et fut endente / oue .iij. seals
pendantz et vn agnys saunz seal et pus a son entre rehercea le count et dit
qil ne / deit a ceo fet respoundre qe la date de ceo fet est vt supra a payer
etc. anno etc. vt supra[1] ou nul tiel terme / poet estre entendu qar la date de
la incarnatioun ala Pasche apres la confeccioun fut autre[2] non obstante[3] /
pur ceo qil change ala nunciacioun auant iugement si a tiel fet qe donne
terme qe ne poet estre entendu / deuoms respoundre. *Bereford* est ceo
vostre fet ou ne mye. *Denom* au fet qe me ne pus lier il ne bosoigne qe /
ieo respounde. *Mutford* vous pledetz bien si le fet fut rasse quasi
diceret si rasure fut troue en paroules portant / charge la court ne
durroit pas foy ne ne chargereyt la partie etc. *Bereford* si ceo ne seit
pas vostre fet il / ne couient pas prouer qil vous puis lyer et pur ceo
il vous couient conustre si vous le voillez voidere et luy / chacea a
conustre ou dedire. *Denom* il ne le poet dedire mes veiez cy aquitaunce de .x. marcz et qaunt a les / autres .x. marcz il mist auant vn
autre aquitaunce. Et qaunt a les .ix. marcz veiez laquitaunce son
general / procurator et resceyuour iugement si rienz etc. *Aldborough*
qaunt a les primers aquitaunces lattorne ne poet dedire et qaunt / a
la terce quei auez vous de ceo qil fut nostre resceyuour. *Denom* prest
etc. qil fut vostre general attourne et procurator / com a receyuoir
vos deners et voz dettes a feare acounte. Et dautre part lescrit voet
a payer a vn assigne / par quei par my cest escrit si auoit il poer a
resceyure et faire acquitaunce. *Aldborough* et nous iugement desicom
vous / auez conu vostre fet demene par quei vous estes oblige et vous
ne moustrez rien qei il auoit qil fut assigne / par nous iugement. Et
ceo qil y auoit vn Agnys pendant saunz seal. *Denom* pur vn autel dit
qil ne / myst pas son seal. *In Crastino Aldborough* com auant demaunda
iugement. *Bereford* bone foy serreyt del houre qe / vous poiez charger
celui qe fut vostre resceyuour par voy dacompte qil seit descharge par
saquittaunce. *Scrope* / il ne couent pas qe vous lessez pur consience
qe vous ne facez ley. *Mutford* pur ceo qe vous auez conu vostre / fet
et ne moustrez nul aquitaunce de cely qe vst powere si agarde la court
qil recouera ses .ix. marcz et ces / damages qe sount taxes par nous a
.xx. souz et en dreit de les .xx. marcz dount vous auez conu qe vous /
estes paye qe vous ne preignetz rien etc. *Mutford* demaunda sil
voilleit suere vers les autres lattorne dit / qe noun eo quod celuy fut

[1] The *vn* of the MS. is obviously a slip for *vt*.
[2–3] For these words another MS. has *neumbre*, which is probably the correct
reading, and I have adopted it in translating.

principal vers qi etc. par qei lescript fut dampne Et sic nota mes qil
vst en / iugement pur luy vers lun les autres respondront ut videtur
quod execucio erit in communi quere processum execucionis Et /
purceo qe touz vssent dedit le fet et troue fut par enqueste nient le
fait cely qe primes respondit et dedit *quere* / si lenqueste coreyt vers
les autres.

DE TERMINO PASCHE ANNO REGNI REGIS EDWARDI

FILII REGIS EDWARDI DUODECIMO

TRANSLATION: PLATE XI

A writ was brought against two [defendants]. One of them said
that at present he had nothing in the freehold. The other said that he
held it by the law of England[1] of the heritage of him who was named
with him [as co-defendant], and he prayed aid of him and was allowed
it; and afterwards he [*i.e.* the co-defendant] joined himself with him
in making answer.

One Master John brought a writ of debt against four [defendants]
by several *precipes* and claimed the whole debt by each *precipe*.

Aldborough counted that [the defendants] wrongly etc., and wrongly
for this reason, that each defendant bound himself in the vill of
St James in the eighth year [of Edward II] to ten marks on the Feast of
St Martin next following, and ten marks at Easter, and nine marks on
the Translation of St Martin, and he tendered a bond which witnessed
that each bound himself in the whole sum, to pay it to this same plaintiff or to his assignee at the aforesaid three terms of the year etc.

Denham imparled and took the deed with him, and it was indented,
with three seals appendant and one lamb-skin tag without a seal, and
afterwards, on his return [into Court] he recapitulated the count and
said that he was under no obligation to put in an answer to this deed,
for the date of this deed is *ut supra* to pay etc. in the year etc. *ut supra*,
and no such term for payment can be understood, for the date of [the
year of] the Incarnation to the Easter after the making of the deed
was another number[2], because it changes at the previous Annunciation[3]. [We ask] judgment whether we need reply to a deed which gives
a term [for payment] which cannot be understood.

Bereford [*J.*]. Is this your deed or not?

Denham. I am not called upon to reply to a deed which cannot bind
me.

Mutford [*J.*]. You would be pleading effectively if there had been
an erasure in the deed—implying that if an erasure had been made
in the charging words the Court would not have had any confidence
[in it] and would not call upon the defendant [to answer it].

Bereford [*J.*]. If this is not your deed you need not show that it

[1] *I.e.* as tenant by the curtesy.
[2] See the text as emended in the footnote.
[3] At this time the new year commenced on March 25th, the Feast of the
Annunciation. Consequently this Easter was not in the same year within
which the instalment was payable.

cannot bind you, and therefore you must say whether you want to defeat it—and he made him either admit it or deny it.

Denham. He [the defendant] cannot deny it; but see here an acquittance for ten marks—and he tendered another acquittance in respect of the other ten marks—and, as to the nine marks, see here the acquittance of his [the plaintiff's] general procurator and receiver. Judgment whether [you can claim] anything etc.

Aldborough. As to the first [two] acquittances, the [plaintiff's] attorney cannot deny them; and, in respect of the third, what have you to prove that he [who gave it] was our receiver?

Denham. Ready [to aver] that he was your general attorney and procurator with authority to receive your moneys and to liquidate your debts. And, further, the writing provides for payment to an assignee, and, consequently, in virtue of this writing he had authority to receive and to give an acquittance.

Aldborough. And we [ask] judgment, seeing that you have acknowledged this to be your own deed by which you are bound, and you offer nothing that [the defendant] has in way of proof that [the granter of the acquittance] was our assignee. Judgment.

And what he had was a lamb-skin tag without a seal.

Denham said, in explanation, that [the maker of the writing] had omitted to put his seal on it.

On the morrow, *Aldborough* asked judgment as before.

Bereford [J.]. Since you can, by way of account, charge him who was your receiver, good faith demands that [the defendant] should be discharged by his acquittance.

Scrope. You must not for conscience sake shirk giving effect to the law.

Mutford [J.]. Since you have acknowledged your deed and show no acquittance from any one who had authority [to give one], the Court gives judgment that [the plaintiff] recover his nine marks and his damages, which are assessed by us at twenty shillings; and that you [*i.e.* the plaintiff] take nothing in respect of the twenty marks which you have admitted that you have been paid.

Mutford [J.] asked if the plaintiff wished to prosecute his claim against the other defendants. The attorney said that he did not, because he was the principal debtor against whom [judgment had been given]; and the writing was therefore annulled. And so note that though the plaintiff had got judgment in his favour against one [of the four defendants], the others might be made answerable; though it seems that [if they were] execution would be given against them in common. See as to the process of execution. And because they had all denied the deed and it had been found by inquest that it was not the deed of him who had first made answer and denied it, *quaere* if an inquest would lie against the others.

[PLEAS] OF THE EASTER-TERM OF THE TWELFTH YEAR OF THE REIGN OF KING EDWARD SON OF KING EDWARD

INDEX OF MATTERS

Tenures of land, in Abingdon, 16
Termes de la Ley, authorship of, 72
Thunderstorm, Court adjourns on
    account of, 98
Tottell's many ways of spelling his
    name, 66
Tower, how the Warden of tne, lost
    his office, 83
Trial by battle, 96

V and W, argument as to the dif-
    ference, if any, between, 105,
    106
Vocabulary, the, of the reporters, 107

Westminster Hall, a description of
    the mediaeval Courts in, 10,
    12, 13
    a jury of the stall-keepers hastily
        empanelled to try an assault
        in, 36
    an estimate of the number of
        people usually there, 35–37
    assault in, by a defendant on
        plaintiff, 36
    'Hell,' a place in, *sub banco*, 37
    stalls in, 36
Westminster II, statute of, drafted by
    Hengham C.J., 31
Wine and beer sold at taverns, com-
    missions to test the, 17

Year Books, the
    Bacon, Lord, on the desirability of
        printing them, 4, 5
    Beginning of, 10
    Coke's knowledge of them, 85
    Commercial syndicate, copies pro-
        bably transcribed for sale by
        a, 54
    Common Law of England and
        America set out in them, 34
    'Corruption, a hopeless mass of,' 3
    Deficiencies of the black-letter
        editions, 6
    Description, brief, of form and
        contents, 32, 33
        of MSS., 41
    Difficulties, presented by the
        script, 44, 55
        in understanding them, 52
    Disuse and oblivion, probable
        reasons why they fell into,
        3, 4
    of Edward II, printed from a MS.
        of Serjeant Maynard, 73

of Edward II, the Table of Con-
    tents appended to, 73
of Eyre of Kent, 78
of Eyres, 38, 77
Folio edition of 1678–1680, 76;
    value of a set in 1678, 74
House of Commons, select com-
    mittee of, on, 5; invites sug-
    gestions, 5; produces first
    report in 1800, 5
Improvements in editing intro-
    duced by Horwood and Pike,
    81, 82
Lincoln's Inn, report by, on MSS., 5
Manuscripts in the Cambridge
    University Library, 39–42
Marginal notes, the, 56–59; may
    have something to reveal, 59
Maynard's, Serjeant, opinion of
    them, 3
Mediaeval literature, light thrown
    on, by, 107
Origin, supposed official, 45
    as suggested in this book, 48–59
    Maitland, Pike and Sir F. Pol-
        lock on the, 47
    Plowden on the, 46
    'Original' one, no, known to exist,
        48
Oxford English Dictionary has no
    examples from them, 102
'Pamphlet Theory,' 54
Printed editions, in the Cambridge
    University Library, 1
    by Machlinia, 63
    by Wynkyn de Worde, 63, 64
    by Rich. Pynson, 64, 65
    by Robt. Redman, 64, 65
    by Rich. Tottell, 66–70
    by John Rastell, 70, 71
    by William ——, 71, 72
    by Company of Stationers, 72
    by various other printers, 72, 73
Quo warranto, writs of, 38
    of Richard II, 78
'Robin Hood in Barnsdale stood,'
    107
Stories in, 19, 30, 83, 94, 95
Work on them by Horwood, 7, 80,
    81
    by Pike, 7, 80, 81
    by the Selden Society, 8, 82
    et passim
Yelverton, Serjeant, offers Serjeant
    Markham forty pence to de-
    mur, 28

INDEX OF PERSONS AND PLACES